D1447034

BEYOND
THE 95 THESES

Martin Luther's Life, Thought,
and Lasting Legacy

Stephen J. Nichols

PUBLISHING
P.O. BOX 817 • PHILLIPSBURG • NEW JERSEY 08865-0817

Permission to use figures 1.2, 1.3, 2.2, 2.3, 3.2, 4.2, 5.1, 6.2, 7.2, 11.2, and 12.1 has been granted by the Richard C. Kessler Reformation Collections of the Pitts Theology Library, Candler School of Theology, Emory University.

Figure 8.1 from Martin Luther, *Lutherifches ABC und Ramen-Buchlein für Kinder* (Philadelphia: Schäfer und Koradi, N.D.); Figure 8.2 from Martin Luther, *Dr. Martin Luther Der kleine Katechismus* (Munich: Müller, 1933); Figure 9.1 originally appeared in Sartain's Union Magazine of Literature and Art, vol. 5, 1849; Figure 10.2 from Moritz Meurer, *The Life of Martin Luther* (New York: H. Ludwig & Co., 1848); Figure 13.1 is from Julius Theodor Kostlin, *Life of Luther* (New York: Scribner's, 1923), 537.

ISBN: 978-1-62995-331-1 (pbk)
ISBN: 978-1-62995-332-8 (ePub)
ISBN: 978-1-62995-333-5 (Mobi)

Printed in the United States of America

Library of Congress Control Number: 2016958703

How do you do a book on everything from training children to sing hymns to preaching to political conflict—and have it running over with the glorious gospel? Nichols has done it. Be alert: people forget how life-changing the gospel really is—and then are astonished to remember it again as they read Luther.

> —**D. Clair Davis**, Emeritus Professor of Church History, Westminster Theological Seminary, Philadelphia

A marvelous mixture of biography, history, theology, and anecdote. If you don't feel the heartbeat of the Reformation in these pages, check your pulse!

> —**Sinclair Ferguson**, Coauthor, *Church History 101*

Stephen Nichols's engaging volume deserves to be widely read, and as an unashamed Luther-lover I hope it will be.

> —**J. I. Packer**, Professor of Theology, Regent College

Nichols has a gift for making a complex subject simple without being simplistic.

> —**Michael A. Rogers**, Senior Pastor, Westminster Presbyterian Church, Lancaster, Pennsylvania

As we celebrate the 500th anniversary of the Reformation, may we not only appreciate the profound ways God used Martin Luther, but may we learn from him. Dr. Nichols gives us a front-row seat on Luther's life. As we watch, may we have the same boldness and the same lifelong commitment to the gospel.

> —**R.C. Sproul**, Founder, Ligonier Ministries

Rarely do we find the rich combination of theological precision and historical passion so accessibly written as we do here in Dr. Nichols' entertaining treatment of Martin Luther. A marvelous introduction.

—**Derek W. H. Thomas**, Professor of Systematic and Pastoral Theology, Reformed Theological Seminary, Atlanta

Those who know nothing of Luther will benefit greatly from such a readable introduction, while those more familiar with him will find Nichol's enthusiasm infectious.

—**Carl B. Trueman**, Professor of Church History, Westminster Theological Seminary, Philadelphia

For Benjamin Hunt Nichols

*May you grow to appreciate and embrace
the rich heritage of Christ's church.*

CONTENTS

List of Illustrations   7

Preface   9

Acknowledgments   13

Introduction: Martin Luther's Legacy   15

Part One: Luther, a Life   23

1. The Early Years: 1483–1521   25
2. The Later Years: 1522–1546   47

Part Two: Luther, the Reformer   67

3. The Meat of the Nut: Understanding Luther's Theology   69
4. Silent No More: The *Three Treatises*   87
5. The Centerpiece of the Reformation: *The Bondage of the Will*   103
6. This Is My Body: *Confession Concerning Christ's Supper*   119
7. Plagues, Princes, and Peasants: Ethical Writings   133

Part Three: Luther, the Pastor   149

8. The Next Generation: *The Small Catechism*   151

Contents

9. Dinner with Luther: "Table Talk"   169
10. A New Song Begun: The Hymns   183
11. The Marks of a True Church: *On the Councils and the Church*   199
12. The Reluctant Pastor: The Sermons   215

Part Four: Luther's *Ninety-Five Theses*   231
13. The Annotated *Ninety-Five Theses:* Disputation on the Power and Efficacy of Indulgences   235

A Brief Guide to Books by and about Martin Luther   263
Bibliography   269
Index of Persons   273
Index of Luther's Works   277
Index of Scripture   281

ILLUSTRATIONS

1.1 Timeline: Early Years   26

1.2 The Seven-Headed Luther (1529)   29

1.3 Title page of Johann von Staupitz's *Examination of Eternal Predestination* (1517)   38

2.1 Timeline: Later Years   48

2.2 Samson Slays a Lion, title page of Luther's pamphlet in response to the Catholic theologians of Louvain   51

2.3 Martin Luther (1546)   58

3.1 The Reformation *Solas*   76

3.2 Title page of Luther's *Commentary on Galatians*   79

4.1 Luther's Decisive Year (1520)   98

4.2 Title page of the Papal Bull issued by Leo X (1520)   100

5.1 Desiderius Erasmus (1466–1536)   105

6.1 Major Writings on the Lord's Supper and Related Events   124

6.2 Ulrich Zwingli (1484–1531)   127

7.1 Major Ethical Writings   135

7.2 Title page of *Whether One May Flee from a Deadly Plague* (1527)   138

8.1 Title page of Luther's *ABC Book for Children*   157
8.2 Title page from a German edition of Luther's *Small Catechism*   161
9.1 Evenings at the Luther Home   177
10.1 "A Mighty Fortress Is Our God"   189
10.2 The Castle at Wartburg   191
11.1 Marks of the True Church   204
11.2 Lutheran Worship Service (ca. 1550)   207
12.1 Lucas Cranach's illustration of Genesis 22 from Luther's German translation of the Bible (1523)   218
13.1 Wittenberg (1546)   233

PREFACE

MARTIN LUTHER stepped out of the Black Cloister in Wittenberg. In this building he and his fellow Augustinian monks, university scholars, and students taught and learned, ate and drank, prayed and slept. Here Martin Luther lived. Here, too, he wrote. He passed through the gate and headed west, guided by the bell tower and steeple of the Schlosskirche, or Castle Church, that rose over the town of Wittenberg. Luther likely could make the trip in his sleep. One kilometer later he arrived at his destination.

Martin Luther had been troubled in the months of 1517. In fact, Martin Luther had been troubled for the past dozen years and, sadly, more years still. In 1505 he had found himself caught in a violent thunderstorm, which he had taken to be nothing less than God's judgment over his soul and God's way of snuffing out his life. Having no alternative, Luther had cut a deal. He would enter the monastery, devoting his life to the quest for piety and peace with God—if only God spared his life from the crashing thunder and streaking lightning.

In the years leading up to 1517, Luther's troubles increased. Peace seemed ever more to elude him. He had high hopes for the church—and at the time there was only one, the Roman Catholic Church—yet he experienced wave upon wave of disillusionment. His trip to Rome, the Holy See, left him utterly deflated.

Then Luther started to hear stories that made his skin crawl and his stomach churn. In the neighboring regions, an indulgence sale was occurring. The Peter Indulgence, as it was called, resulted from a deal struck by Albert, Archbishop of Mainz, and Pope Leo X. Unprecedented, the indulgence offered purchasers a free pass to paradise, no need to stop in purgatory. It also offered release from purgatory for one's relatives, one's suffering relatives. All one had to do was throw a coin into the coffer.

That summer, Luther managed to get a copy of "The Summary Instruction." This document, prepared by Albert and his theologians, gave explicit instructions to the indulgence sale preachers—Luther called them "hawkers." The document was troubling enough, as it made a mockery of church law. What made the matter far worse was that Luther's own parishioners from Wittenberg were traveling to Albert's region, purchasing indulgences, and spiraling downward in their lives. What incentive did they have to do otherwise? They had their indulgence. They had their Get Out of Jail Free card.

Luther poignantly felt the strain. The indulgence had the Pope's seal of approval, yet it was patently without warrant. Luther's inward tensions mounted as he could not help but see the damage being done.

As fall came to Wittenberg, the air grew crisper, and the leaves changed their colors, Luther could be silent no more. He was a Doctor of Sacred Theology. He was a priest. He had training, and he held a position that obligated him to serve the church, even if that meant calling the church out. So he filled his inkwell, sat at his desk, and set to work.

By the time he finished writing, he had ninety-five

separate arguments and observations on the indulgence sale. He readied himself for a debate. He wrote a letter to Albert, Archbishop of Mainz, that same day. Luther planned to post the letter along with a copy of his theses where his fellow Wittenberg scholars could engage the debate. He took his copy and a mallet and headed west out the gate to the Castle Church doors.

Five hundred years later, we celebrate this moment in history—for it made history. What Luther did on that last day of October in 1517 started the Protestant Reformation, impacting both church and culture for five full centuries and counting. It was truly a remarkable event, executed by one of history's most colorful figures.

The posting of the *Ninety-Five Theses* to the church door stands as the epochal moment in Luther's life. But it does not stand alone. Other defining moments would come after October 31, 1517. Much more would flow from Luther's quill and inkwells than the *Ninety-Five Theses*.

This book offers a guided tour of Martin Luther's life, writings, and thought. It is offered not in the hope that we merely enshrine Luther and his legacy but that in the hope that we too might find the same confidence in God, the Mighty Fortress; in God's sure and certain Word; and in Christ and his finished work on the cross—alone. May we look back and be filled with gratitude for Luther's life and legacy.

May we also look ahead. If Christ delays his return and the church sees the year 2517, will there be cause to celebrate our acts and our legacy?

Our celebration of the past reminds us of our obligation in the present and our commitment to the future. Looking ahead seems to be the best way to celebrate the five-hundredth anniversary of Martin Luther's posting of the *Ninety-Five Theses*.

ACKNOWLEDGMENTS

I AM GRATEFUL TO my friends at P&R Publishing, including Bryce Craig, Amanda Martin, and Ian Thompson. Thank you for your support of this new edition. I am also thankful for my colleagues at Ligonier and at Reformation Bible College. I have long wished that I could travel back in time and have just one meal with Luther. Working with R.C. Sproul is close enough. Caleb Gorton, Anthony Salangsang, Megan Taylor, Emberlee van Eyk, and Jeanna Will all helped to get this to the finish line. Without the kind encouragement of Chris Larson, this new edition likely would not have happened.

Luther was above all a family man, and so I am grateful to my family for their unstinting love. Thank you.

INTRODUCTION

Martin Luther's Legacy

I N SHEER TERROR, he made a vow to his patron saint. In disillusionment, he questioned the practices of the church to which he gave his very life. In firm resolve, he nailed his list of protests to the church door. In utter joy, he grasped the liberating idea that the righteousness of God is given, not earned. And in the face of intense spiritual battle, he cried out to God, his "mighty fortress," his "bulwark never failing." These are the defining moments of Martin Luther's life. Most, if not all, Christians know these defining moments. Most also know that with every mallet swing on the church door at Wittenberg, Luther sparked the Protestant Reformation. But much more, these events also serve to shape our lives, as well, for they embody the Reformation and form the foundation of Protestantism. One historian has even remarked that any vestige of Christianity in Western culture is entirely owing to this man, Martin Luther.

Yet, while Luther is very well known, beyond some significant moments, much of his life remains a mystery to most Christians. And while his writings form the bedrock of Protestantism and articulate the essential principles of Reformation theology, they largely go unread by many today. This current lack of familiarity with Luther's work is precisely the reason for this book. It is an attempt to put his long-lost descendants in touch with their legacy, an invitation to spend some time at Luther's table, to examine his life and hear his ideas. These ideas, however, are not mere relics of the past. To be sure, his thought inspired a whole generation in his own day. But, it also has the power to impact the church today and to ignite our own generation to a passionate quest for God and his truth. Biographies of Luther abound, and specialized works on his thought fill many bookshelves. His own writings continue to be published centuries after his death. With all of this attention given to Luther, one may rightly ask why. What is it about Luther that demands so much attention?

Luther's Legacy

Luther's role as the catalyst of the Reformation stands at the forefront of reasons for the perennial interest in him. Imagine a world without Protestantism. If you were a young Augustinian monk in the early decades of the sixteenth century, this is actually not such a difficult situation to imagine. For Luther, reality was a world without Protestantism. His choices were clear: either the Roman Catholic Church or paganism. As a monk, of course, he embraced the former. When Luther died in 1546, however, the world had changed drastically. Between Roman Catholicism and paganism now lay a whole range of choices including Lutheranism, Anabaptism, Reformed, Anglicanism, and Presbyterianism. These religious options were simply not the case in 1517. In that year, Luther initiated a sea change of reform that would shake the entire world.

Before Luther's challenge to the church, various attempts

at reform had occurred. Some movements, such as the *Devotio Moderna* (New Devotion), criticized the lackadaisical spirituality, as well as the enormous wealth, of the church. Though its objections ran deep, the movement lacked a theological base from which to mount its critique. Other movements, though more theologically oriented, did not succeed in overhauling the church either. John Wycliffe in England and John Hus in Bohemia (the modern-day Czech Republic) mounted formidable challenges, but finally were crushed by Rome's power. Hus was burned at the stake, and while Wycliffe died of natural causes, the church, nevertheless, exhumed his body and burned his bones.

Though these pre-Reformation reformers did not bring about lasting reformation, they laid an important foundation upon which Luther built. In fact, Luther recognized these pre-Reformation reformers' invaluable contributions. From Wycliffe, Luther realized the importance of placing the Bible in the people's hands in a language they could understand. From Hus, Luther learned to challenge the various church practices and functions that were opposed to Scripture. From the *Devotio Moderna*, Luther also understood that the church's lack of spiritual vigor should be challenged. Yet, unlike this movement, he knew that such a challenge must be built upon a theological foundation. In fact, as he debates Erasmus over the will, Luther underscores that the central concern for the church is a theological one. Take away doctrine, Luther argues, and you have no church.

Luther grew skeptical of the church's basic theological understanding from the mid-1510s when he began lecturing on the Psalms, Romans, Galatians, and Hebrews at Wittenberg. His first salvo against the church, however, came as he contemplated the severe problems caused by indulgences. This error, of course, led to the posting of the *Ninety-Five Theses* at Wittenberg. Through this event, and also his recovery of the doctrine of justification by faith, his courageous stand before both the church and empire at the Diet of Worms, and his tireless commitment to building a church upon Scripture alone, Luther served as the Reformation's architect. His work at Wittenberg rippled across the German lands and throughout Europe. By the time of his death, Protestantism and the new evangelical church were firmly established.

Secondly, Luther garners attention not solely for his involvement in Reformation events, but also because of his role in shaping Reformation ideas. Perhaps more than any other person, Luther shaped the presuppositions that define Protestantism. Theologians use a series of Latin expressions to capture these concepts. Known as the "Reformation *Solas*," they include *sola Scriptura*, Scripture alone; *sola fide*, faith alone; *sola gratia*, grace alone; *solus Christus*, Christ alone; and *soli Deo gloria*, to the glory of God alone. These ideas all take root in Martin Luther's thinking. That they continue to define Christianity is a lasting testimony to Luther's influence.

Luther also attracts attention because of his colorful personality. "Indiscretion," Luther once remarked, is "said to be my greatest fault." Consequently, both his writings and actions are humorous, poignant, and vivid. His colorful personality extends to his conversations and writing. Reading through his "Table Talk" selections will undoubtedly cause some to blush on occasion. Further, when it came to engaging his enemies, Luther seldom showed restraint in his language. In some sense, these are not necessarily positive traits. Nevertheless, Luther's transparent demeanor and, at times, candidness provide numerous anecdotes and vignettes that continue to fascinate readers today. Historical figures sometimes may be one-dimensional to later generations of readers. We may piece together a sense of the person through various accounts, but typically we see the personal portrait dimly.

This is not the case with Luther. And the portrait of Luther that emerges, despite his peccadilloes, is rather endearing.

Friedrich Nietzsche, a German Lutheran, at least at one point in his life, once said that we are "human, all too human." This sentiment describes Luther, as well. Hailed by the German artist Hans Holbein as the "German Hercules," Luther appeared to many as larger than life. Yet, in reality, while he had legs of iron, he nevertheless had feet of clay. Perhaps the most prominent fault in Luther is reflected in his harsh attitude toward the Jews later in his life. Rather than hide these faults, or overemphasize them, we are better served simply to acknowledge them. Despite Holbein's depiction, Luther was human. This is not to excuse his faults, either. Rather, it reminds us that while we admire Luther, we must also see him as a sinner saved by grace.

Finally, Luther's tireless commitment to the church assures him a prominent place in its history. He showed remarkable versatility, courage at defining moments, and stamina to endure the long haul. Rarely do we see the combination of the visionary who also implements his vision. Luther's life offers one of the rare cases. Not only did he take a bold stand and point the church in the right direction, he committed his life to leading the church in the right path. Luther worked tirelessly, and often at a great personal sacrifice, to see that the church thrived in his lifetime and beyond. These reasons, and others, substantiate the widespread attention that Luther receives. In the chapters that follow, we will continue to explore why Luther not only receives such attention, but also why he deserves it.

Overview

We begin our tour of Martin Luther by taking account of his eventful life. In chapter 1 we trace the steps of his early life along the road to the Protestant Reformation. After his education, and a traumatic experience during a thunderstorm, Luther enters the monastery. Roughly a dozen years later, the pope declares him a heretic. Following the decisive confrontation at the Diet of Worms, Luther enters his "exile" at the Wartburg Castle. In chapter 2 we continue his life's narrative, beginning with his return to Wittenberg and ending with the last decades of his life.

Part 2 presents various discussions on Luther, the reformer. In chapter 3 we offer an overview of his theology. The next chapter engages the *Three Treatises*, pivotal texts from the fall months of 1520. Luther's theological magnum opus, *The Bondage of the Will*, is the focus of chapter 5, addressing what Luther called the "vital spot" of the Reformation. Here we explore this crucial text as it unfolds Luther's understanding of the human will and God's sovereignty. In chapter 6, we examine the Lord's Supper and the role that it played in the Reformation. Part 2 comes to a close as we look at Luther's thought and writings on ethics. Some key historical events in his day, such as the Peasants' War and the plague at Wittenberg, enable us to see Luther's thought applied.

Luther devoted the majority of his energies to the church's theology and practice. In Part 3, we continue our tour of Luther's life and thought by examining his contributions to church life. *The Small Catechism*, the subject of chapter 7, endures as a testimony to Luther's realization of the church's role in properly training the next generation. Chapter 8 looks at a unique text in church history, Luther's "Table Talk." Here Luther transparently lives out his theology before his family, colleagues, and students, as they all gather around his dinner table. Because of the foresight of both Luther and some student scribes, we can listen in on those conversations. While we all know Luther's hymn "A Mighty Fortress Is Our

God," we may not be familiar with the prominent place music played in his life. Chapter 10 provides an opportunity to delve into this part of Luther's experience. In chapter 11, we explore Luther's ideas regarding the "true church" by studying one of his lesser-known, but profound, texts, *On the Councils and the Church*. Finally, Luther left behind an enormous amount of sermon material. We examine one sermon in particular, "On How to Contemplate Christ's Holy Suffering," as representative of his approximately 6,000 sermons.

Overall this book introduces both the life and thought of Martin Luther. It is not intended as an exhaustive treatment of either. Ideally, it would be helpful to include many more texts and issues to show Luther in all his genius. Practically, however, that would try the patience of reader and writer alike. The most comprehensive collection of Luther's writings in English fills fifty-five volumes, which only covers approximately half of his work. Consequently, I have chosen the texts and concerns that seem pivotal in Luther's thought. This book, then, is intended as an acquaintance with Luther which will serve as the gateway for further exploration of his life and thought. The conclusion offers some suggestions and guidance for continuing your journey.

Following Luther's death, his close friend the artist Lucas Cranach painted one last portrait of the reformer. Cranach captured Luther's entire life and purpose in this three-paneled painting, which was installed at the Castle Church in Wittenberg. The right panel depicts Luther in the pulpit, proclaiming the Word of God, as he faithfully shepherds his flock. With an open Bible before him, he stands pointing to his congregation. On the left panel, an assembled congregation listens intently to the reformer. Cranach painted Luther's wife Katie, a son, and even his daughter Magdalena, who had died a few years before, into the congregation. They are not, however, looking directly at Luther. The center panel depicts Christ on the cross. Taken collectively, the three panels poignantly express Luther's passion as he points to Christ for all to see. More specifically, as they look to Luther, he points them to Christ. So I offer this book which, although it points to Luther, directs us to Christ. Ultimately, that is Martin Luther's legacy.

PART ONE

LUTHER, A LIFE

ARTIN LUTHER lived an eventful life; consequently, the question of what to leave out becomes every Luther biographer's major challenge. With only two chapters specifically devoted to biography, we especially face that challenge. Nevertheless, I have attempted to address the crucial events in Luther's life. These incidents, explored in chapter 1, include such pivotal moments as the vow made during the thunderstorm that sent him to the monastery, the posting of the *Ninety-Five Theses* that catapulted him to the very center of everyone's attention in 1517, and the Reformation discovery of *justification by faith* that "opened the very gates of paradise" for him and that became the fundamental message of all he preached. This chapter ends with Luther's bold stand before the Diet of Worms and then describes his "kidnapping."

In the next chapter, we pick up the story as Luther returns from his exile at the Wartburg Castle. The events unfolding during these later years include the marriage of this former monk to a former nun, the establishment of the first parsonage in the modern age, the decisive meeting with theologian Ulrich Zwingli at Marburg, and the tireless commitment to establishing the newly formed church. Through studying the events of both his early and later years, we begin to understand why Luther figures so prominently in the pages of history, and why he continues to fascinate readers five centuries after his death.

1

THE EARLY YEARS

1483–1521

"If there is any sense remaining of Christian civilization in the West, this man Luther in no small measure deserves the credit."
Roland Bainton

"Martin Luther the Reformer is one of the most extraordinary persons in history and has left a deeper impression of his presence in the modern world than any other except Columbus."
Ralph Waldo Emerson

I N 1529 JOHANNES COCHLAEUS authored a tract vilifying Martin Luther. Entitled the "Seven-Headed Luther," the piece featured a woodcut on the title page caricaturing Luther as a dangerously conflicted individual who, according to the writer, threatened great harm to the church through his varied and contradictory personalities. One portrayal depicts Luther as a madman with bees encircling his head. The final woodcut depicts him as Barabbas, implying no less than the charge that he was the very enemy of Christ.

Pope Leo X, who originally viewed Luther's antics as nothing more than the ravings of a drunken German, portrayed Luther as the archenemy of the church, and he succeeded in rallying both church and empire against the German monk. Even at Luther's death many wondered about his true legacy. Was he an instrument of God? Or, was he a tool in the hands of the devil?

One thing on which scholars agree is that the world "Martin Luder" was born into on November 10, 1483, was quite different from the one he left on February 18, 1546. The decades of his life contained unprecedented change

Fig. 1.1 Timeline: Early Years

1483	Born on November 10 in Eisleben
1492-98	Attends school at Mansfield, Magdeburg, and Eisenach
1501-05	Attends University of Erfurt; receives B.A. (1502), M.A. (1505)
1505	Makes vow during thunderstorm, July 2. Enters monastery
1507	Is ordained
1509	Receives B.A. in Bible. Begins lecturing at Erfurt on the arts
1510	Makes pilgrimage to Rome
1511	Enters Black Cloister, Augustinian Monastery at Wittenberg
1512	Receives doctorate in theology. Appointed to faculty of theology at Wittenberg
1513-17	Lectures on Psalms, Romans, Galatians, and Hebrews
1517	Posts *Ninety-Five Theses* on church door on October 31
1518	Debates Cajetan at Augsburg
1518-19	Possible date for Reformation breakthrough (or 1515-16)
1519	Debates Eck at Leipzig
1520	Writes *Three Treatises*
1520	Receives Papal Bull
1521	Appears at Diet of Worms on April 16-18
1521	Is placed under the Imperial Ban and condemned as a heretic and outlaw in May
1521	Goes into "exile" at Wartburg Castle

and upheaval, and Martin Luther was at the center of it all. Luther, however, experienced quite modest beginnings for such an enduringly prominent figure in Western history. As he wrote in his old age, "I come from a family of peasants." In fact, he continued:

> Who would have divined that I would receive a Bachelor's and then a Master's of Arts, then lay aside my brown student's cap and leave it to others in order to become monk, thereby of course earning for myself such shame so that my father was bitterly displeased; and that despite all I would get in the Pope's hair—and he in mine—and take a runaway nun for my wife? Who would have predicted this for me?

Luther's Early Education

Few would have predicted the outcome of Luther's life, especially his parents. Hans and Margaret Luder moved from Eisleben, Germany, the place of Luther's birth and baptism, to Mansfield in Luther's first year. At Mansfield, Hans continued his work as a miner, overseeing two smelting furnaces, painstakingly providing for young Martin's education. Instead of working as a young boy, the lot of most peasant youth, Luther attended school where he studied Latin, elementary grammar, and the essentials of a religious education—the Ten Commandments, the Lord's Prayer, and the children's creeds. Here he opted for the Latinized version of his name, Luther, instead of the German, Luder. When Luther turned fourteen, his parents sent him to continue his education at the monastery in Magdeburg. This monastery fell under the jurisdiction of the Brethren of the Common Life order, known for its piety, and counting among its members Thomas á Kempis, the author of the devotional classic

The Imitation of Christ. Magdeburg was a highly respected school and, consequently, very expensive. The Luther family's modest income barely funded Martin's first year, so, like the other peasant students, he took to begging in the street for his bread. "Panem propter Deum," bread for God's sake, rolled off Luther's tongue often as he begged along the streets of Magdeburg.

The next year Luther continued his studies at Eisenach. Presumably, Eisenach appealed to Luther for both academic and financial reasons. Luther's mother had relatives nearby who undoubtedly offered some relief, as well as occasional meals. It was, however, an elderly town lady who, admiring Luther's abilities and resolve, took special care of him. Even with this help, Luther's time at Eisenach was a struggle. Despite these challenges, he excelled in his studies, rising to the head of the class. His achievements allowed him to move on to Erfurt where he could study law to fulfill his parents' dream for their son's life. Through entering a noble profession, his parents hoped he would escape the peasant class and bring honor and status to the family name. At Erfurt, he received his Bachelor's degree in 1502, and his Master's in 1505. Both were to prepare him for further study of the law and a doctorate in jurisprudence.

I Will Become a Monk

Studying at Erfurt was a turning point in Luther's life on many levels. On his daily walk, he encountered a sculpture that often captured his thoughts. The image depicts Christ as judge with a sword clenched between his teeth and a piercing stare. This image, not only in medieval renderings of Christ, haunted Luther for years as he contemplated his guilt before God. A particular German word helps us understand the true impact of this image on Luther's life: *anfechtung.* Translated as "crisis" or "struggle," in Luther's case it is best described as an intense spiritual struggle and a crisis. In fact, it is better to use the word in the plural, *anfechtungen*, for in reality a series of spiritual crises marked Luther's early life of study.

After completing his M.A. in January 1505, Luther remained at Erfurt to receive specialized training in law. He excelled in the legal field and was well on his way to fulfilling

1.2 Not all responses to Luther were favorable. This depiction of Luther as a seven-headed monster graces the title page of Johannes Cochlaeus's 1529 book criticizing Luther.

his father's wish. In June of that year, he made a trip home to Mansfield. On his return to Erfurt Luther was caught in a violent thunderstorm. He was paralyzed by the storm and attached great spiritual significance to it, and in utter fear he believed God had unleashed the very thunder of heaven to judge his soul. In total desperation he cried out to St. Anne, the patron saint of miners: "Help me, St. Anne, and I will become a monk." The date was July 2, 1505. Exactly two weeks later, Luther threw a party for his classmates, giving them his law books and his master's cap and withdrawing from his doctoral studies. Then he told them that on the following day he would enter the monastery.

Luther desired his father's blessing for exchanging the master's cap for the monk's tunic; the blessing, however, did not come. As Luther records, "When I became a monk, my father almost went out of his mind. He was all upset and refused to give me his permission." Later, in 1521, Luther apologized for disobeying his parents in his dedicatory letter to *On Monastic Vows*, addressed to his father. Fifteen years before the book, and despite his parents' refusal, Luther entered the monastery. All candidates were accepted on probation for one year's time. During this time, as a "novice," Luther threw himself into the rigors of monastic life and completed his year of probation. He took the monk's habit in 1506 during a ceremony which culminated in Luther's prostrating himself before the abbot. Ironically this was over the very slab that covered the grave of a principal accuser of reformer John Hus. And on the slab was that haunting image of Christ as judge. His parents did not respond to the invitation to attend the ceremony. Luther hoped that by entering the monastery he would resolve his spiritual crises. In reality, however, it only fueled them. One year after his vow to St. Anne, Luther was abandoned by his family, and he also acutely felt abandoned by God.

In later years, Luther reflected back on his life as a monk: "I myself was a monk for twenty years. I tortured myself with praying, fasting, keeping vigils, and freezing—the cold alone was enough to kill me—and I inflicted upon myself such pain as I would never inflict again, even if I could." In fact, Luther carried out his duties with such rigor that he exclaimed, "If any monk ever got to heaven by monkery, then I should have made it. All my monastery companions who knew me can testify to that." He concludes his reminiscing by noting that "if it had lasted much longer, I would have killed myself with vigils, praying, reading, and the other labors." But, there was still no resolution to his spiritual crises.

As the first decade of the sixteenth century came to a close, two occurrences profoundly impacted the young monk and set him on a course that would revolutionize the church. His prior, or superior, at Erfurt often expressed to the abbott, Johann von Staupitz, his exasperation with young Martin Luther. Staupitz, though confounded by Luther's spiritual struggles, recognized the young man's intellectual abilities and promise. He ordered Luther transferred to the monastery at Wittenberg. Just a few years earlier, Staupitz and others founded the University at Wittenberg. Frederick the Wise spared no expense in making his new university rival the already established universities covering German lands and beyond. He wanted the best and brightest faculty, and he wholeheartedly approved of the choice of Luther. Luther's training, however, was not in Bible and theology; consequently, before he began his career as a lecturer in Bible and theology, he once again became a student. While studying at Wittenberg, he lectured on both the arts and Aristotle. Staupitz hoped that the mental occupations of academia would crowd out Luther's many internal struggles. He was wrong.

Luther began his second set of degrees, taking another B.A. in Bible in 1509. He was then sent back to Erfurt to be a lecturer. While there, the monastery at Erfurt needed to send some documents to Rome. Staupitz viewed this request as an opportunity for Luther to make his peace with God, believing the Holy City would do his soul much good. Luther and another monk embarked on their pilgrimage to Rome in 1510, traveling the same route as thousands of monks over the centuries of the medieval era. Anticipating a spiritual paradise, Luther instead discovered something much more akin to John Bunyan's "Vanity Fair" in *Pilgrim's Progress*. "When I first saw Rome," he recalls, "I fell to the ground, lifted my hands, and said, Hail to thee, O Holy Rome." That impression quickly dissolved, however. He continues, "No one can imagine the knavery, the horrible sinfulness and debauchery that are rampant in Rome." As he climbed up and down the stairs of Pontius Pilate, reciting the Lord's Prayer on each step, his disillusionment only increased. By the time he reached the top, he exclaimed, "Who knows if this is true?"

The trip to Rome failed to quell the storms of Luther's soul. On one occasion, after his return, Luther met up with Staupitz in the garden at the Wittenberg cloister. Staupitz did not understand why Luther could not comprehend God's love for him. "Love God?" Luther retorted, "I can't love God, I hate him." Staupitz had no solution for the young man, other than to order him to pursue a doctorate in theology. Again, he argued that studying the church fathers and the medieval tradition would end his fight with God. In 1512, Luther received his doctorate, not in his originally intended course of law, but in theology, and joined the faculty in that subject at Wittenberg.

Scholar at Wittenberg

While Luther did not know it at the time, this prescription of more education precisely fit the bill, though it did not serve to dispel the dark spiritual clouds immediately. In fact, life was going to get worse before it got better. Luther plunged into his lectures and doctoral work, beginning with Peter Lombard's *Four Books of Sentences* (1158). This systematic and logical treatment of doctrine served as the textbook in theology from 1200 until Luther's day and beyond. This work was so influential it needed to be mastered to qualify for a doctoral degree in medieval universities. Something in Luther's reading of Lombard turned his attention to Augustine. In the margin notes of his copy of the *Sentences*, Luther scribbled numerous references to the great ancient church father. And as he turned to focus on Augustine, he was immediately led by Augustine to Paul. Luther's marginal notes also show that this aspiring theologian encountered difficulties reconciling what he read in Paul and Augustine with Lombard and some of the church's teaching in the high and later Middle Ages. Specifically, the issues of the human will and of sin perplexed Luther. The notes also show that he, nevertheless, affirmed medieval Catholic conceptions of faith and salvation. But as early as 1512, Luther was beginning to part ways with Rome on these latter two issues.

These questions slowly boiled until 1517 and the aftermath experienced after Luther posted the *Ninety-Five Theses* on the Wittenberg door. In the intervening years, he continued his work at Wittenberg, teaching, preaching, praying, and yet all the while doubting, probing, and questioning. In addition to his lectures on theology from Lombard's *Sentences*, he prepared lectures on the Psalms (1513–1515), and then on Romans, Galatians, and Hebrews (1515–1518). In these lectures, Luther reflected the humanism of the sixteenth century. This new approach is not to be confused with the secular humanism of our day. Humanism expressed the Renaissance spirit emphasizing a return to Greek and Roman cultures. It was, in many ways, a reactionary movement against the medieval traditions. That approach, called scholasticism, underscored the later Latin fathers and Aristotle's thought. Scholasticism emphasized the medieval commentaries on Aristotle—and even the commentaries on the commentaries—rather than Aristotle's writings primarily. Like scaffolding around a building, these commentaries blocked a direct line to the sources themselves. Humanism proposed moving beyond the scaffolding with the battlecry, "*Ad Fontes*," "to the fount," or "to the source." And in this spirit, Luther went beyond the scaffolding that obstructed the Bible and went straight to the biblical text.

Once Luther went to the text, he continued encountering difficulties reconciling Scripture with the church's teaching. In his work on the Psalms, like the other medieval exegetes, or interpreters, he applied much of the text, especially the kingly elements, to Christ. Unlike the others, however, he also applied the suffering and servile elements to Christ. For Luther, Christ was seen in both his majesty and humility, as high and low, as king and beggar. Only the majestic side of Christ appealed to the medieval Roman Church leaders. A few years later, this difference between Luther and the church widened even further as Luther articulated his theology as a "theology of the cross" over against a "theology of glory." Not only was he thinking about Christ differently than his contemporaries, but he also began thinking differently about sin and salvation as evidenced in his work on Romans, Galatians, and Hebrews.

His thoughts on sin and salvation will be explored more in later chapters, but for now a brief mention of his key ideas will help us see the progression of his thought. The first concept involves an understanding of sin that moves beyond individual sins one may commit. As Luther understands Paul, our sin is like the root of a plant; just as the root is at the very core of the plant and permeates it, so is sin in our lives. Luther even uses the Latin word for root, *radix*, as a vivid word picture of our true nature as sinners at the root. The upshot of his understanding is that forgiveness and redemption will have to move beyond the mere individual sins that we commit and address our very nature as sinners. This realization stands in stark conflict with the medieval penitential and confessional system based on individual sins.

As for salvation, the key idea that Luther begins to explore concerns "alien righteousness." This term simply means that the righteousness that God requires as our righteous judge cannot be produced by us because we are sinners at the root. This righteousness must come from outside of us; consequently, it is alien to us and not inherent within us. It would be a few years until these ideas reached a full crescendo for Luther, but even as early as 1516 his thinking was headed toward the Reformation's great principle of *sola fide*, or justification by faith alone. And with this understanding, Luther was headed in a direction far from Rome.

The *Ninety-Five Theses*

During these years, Luther is center stage at one of the most significant events in Western history: the posting of the *Ninety-Five Theses* to the church door at Wittenberg on October 31, 1517. In his preface to this document, Luther explained his motives: "Out of love for the truth and the desire to bring it to light, the following propositions will be discussed at Wittenberg, under the oversight of the Reverend Father Martin Luther . . . [who] requests that those who are unable to be present and debate orally with us, may do so by letter." Luther never got his debate; the *Ninety-Five Theses*, originally written in Latin, were quickly translated and distributed around Germany and beyond. A copy reached Pope Leo X, who dismissed the document as nothing more than the ramblings of a drunken German who, he believed, would think differently when sober. The issue of the *Ninety-Five Theses*, a series of short propositions presented for an argument, concerns indulgences and the specific sale of indulgences by the monk, Tetzel.

Tetzel was on a mission for Albert of Mainz. Albert already had exceeded the boundaries of canon law by holding two bishoprics as he sought to become Archbishop of Mainz. Leo X, the pope at the time, granted the necessary papal dispensation, but it also came at a cost. Leo X, of the Medici family of Florence, was a passionate patron of the arts. Determined that his legacy, the great Sistine Chapel of St. Paul's Basillica, be unparalleled, he enlisted the assistance of artists such as Raphael, Durer, and Michelangelo. This commitment, of course, cost a great deal and drained the church treasuries. Consequently, Albert could have his Archbishopric if he provided the funds first. Albert's great wealth consisted largely of land holdings rather than currency, but Tetzel devised a scheme to raise the necessary funds.

To understand indulgences, we need to become acquainted with the system of penance for the Roman church. Penance involved four steps: contrition, confession, satisfaction, and absolution. Tetzel's indulgence, which came with Leo X's seal of approval, short-circuited the process by reducing the first three steps down to one quite simple one: the purchase of an indulgence slip. With the indulgence, Tetzel assured his purchasers, comes full absolution or "complete forgiveness of all sins." Tetzel offered indulgences for oneself and also for one's dead relatives suffering in purgatory. His indulgences found a ready market and also one very irate monk. When Luther heard of the indulgences and of how parishioners from Wittenberg were making the short trek to Mainz to purchase them, as well, he feverishly penned the *Ninety-Five Theses*. Luther clearly had Tetzel in view as he referred to the "hawkers of indulgences" and the "lust and license of the indulgence preachers." He was also well aware of Tetzel's ulterior motive and sought to expose it: "Christians are to be taught that if the pope knew the exactions of the indulgence preachers, he would rather that St. Peter's church should go to the ashes, than that it should be built up with the skin, flesh and bones of his sheep."

Thesis 53 further explains why this stance caused such problems for Luther: "They are the enemies of Christ and the pope, who bid the Word of God to be silent in some churches, in order that pardons be preached in others." The indulgence sale tied Luther's hands. How could he preach about doing good works and following Scripture if his parishioners had simply to pull out their indulgence slips? Luther argued primarily against indulgences based on the church's understanding of penance. He later wrote, "I certainly thought in this case I should have a protector in the pope, on whose trustworthiness I then leaned strongly, for in his decrees he most clearly damned the immoderation of the indulgence preachers." Sadly, Luther never received Leo X's support; instead, this action started Luther down a path that would lead him far from Rome. At this point, and even for the next two years, Luther desired to reform the church within, as he had no intention of breaking with it altogether. As Luther's theological understanding developed, however, he soon realized the impossibility of that approach.

The Reformation Discovery

Luther scholars disagree on the exact date of the reformer's conversion. Suggestions range from 1513 to 1520. Most likely Luther was converted in either 1515–1516 or 1518. The evidence in favor of the earlier date consists largely of some of his comments in his Romans lectures. Evidence in favor of a 1518 date includes some of his comments in the *Ninety-Five Theses* that are not consistent with an understanding of justification by faith. This holds more weight when we consider how Luther, in his later years, regretted these writings for their content. Secondly, Luther's own testimony of the Reformation discovery, given in 1545 in the preface to the Latin edition of his collected works, dates the discovery to 1518. Luther recalls that it was after he had given his lectures on Romans, Galatians, and Hebrews and was giving his second series of lectures on the Psalms, which occurred in 1518.

1.3 Johann von Staupitz, Luther's mentor, published his work on predestination in 1517.

While Luther's conversion date is debated, the nature of his conversion itself remains remarkable. For Luther, real faith meant coming to grips with the righteousness of God in Romans 1:17, where Paul exclaims that in the gospel "a righteousness from God is revealed, a righteousness that is by faith from first to last, just as it is written, 'The righteous will live by faith.' " As Luther reflected on the righteousness of God, he did not embrace it; rather, he states, "I hated the righteous God who punishes sinners. . . . Thus I raged with a fierce and troubled conscience." He hated the righteousness of God because he understood it to mean that which he had to achieve. His breakthrough, the resolution to his long-endured spiritual struggles, came when, "by the mercy of God," he finally realized that the righteousness that Paul refers to and that God requires is not something that we have to earn, but is something that Christ accomplished for us. So he explains:

> There I began to understand that the righteousness of God is that by which the righteous lives by a gift of God, namely by faith. And this is the meaning: The righteousness of God is revealed by the gospel, namely the passive righteousness with which the merciful God justifies us by faith. . . . Here I felt that I was altogether born again and had entered paradise itself through open gates.

As a result, Luther exchanged his anger toward God for love. He wrote, "I extolled that sweetest word with a love as great as the hatred with which I had before hated the word 'righteousness of God.' " Luther moved from viewing righteousness as active, as something he had to achieve, to viewing it as passive, something Christ achieved on his behalf, apprehended not by our merits but by faith alone. The Reformation plank of *sola fide,* faith alone, was born, and Luther was born again.

Debates with Rome

In the aftermath of writing the *Ninety-Five Theses* and his conversion, Luther was summoned to Rome to account for his antics. But by using Frederick the Wise's influence, he avoided going to Rome. Had he gone, he may never have returned; instead, he was summoned to Augsburg in the middle of October 1518 to debate Cardinal Cajetan. More an inquisition than a debate, the meeting met with little success. Both parties talked past each other. Luther stressed the authority of Scripture and salvation by faith. Neither of these points were understood, much less persuasive, for Cajetan. Cajetan's goal was to force Luther to recant his writings and ideas or acquire evidence to have him condemned as a heretic. While it was clear to Cajetan that Luther was a radical, he was unable to extract any clear comments from the reformer that would condemn him as a heretic. Luther left the meeting unsure of what moves the church would make next; Cajetan left without a recantation or a heretic.

Luther met a much more formidable opponent in his Leipzig debate in 1519 with Johann Eck, a trained theologian who taught at the prestigious University of Ingolstadt. Eck began writing against Luther as soon as the first copies of the *Ninety-Five Theses* rolled off the press. Officially, the debate was between Eck and Luther's senior colleague in theology from Wittenberg, Andreas Karlstadt. In reality, the debate was between Eck and Luther. Eck used an effective strategy: he aligned Luther with Wycliffe and Hus, both condemned as heretics. Luther, consequently, became guilty simply by association. For Luther, however, the debate provided a platform to expound his doctrine of the authority of Scripture, known as *sola Scriptura*, or Scripture alone. Luther's commitment to the Scripture's authority over the church fathers, councils, and even the Pope resounded throughout the debate. At one point, Luther went so far as to claim that even a simple schoolboy armed with the text is better equipped than the Pope himself.

This debate, unlike the one with Cajetan, left little ambiguity as to the outcome; Martin Luther was outside of conformity with the church. But he was not declared a heretic yet. Eck, however, diligently worked to that end and in 1520 obtained the papal bull that officially declared Luther the enemy of the church, the enemy of the apostles, and the very enemy of Christ. Entitled *"Exsurge, Domine,"* "Arise, O Lord," Leo X's bull issued on June 15, 1520, called for the immediate restraint of the "wild boar in God's vineyard." It gave Luther, the wild boar, no alternative: he had but sixty days after receiving the bull to recant. If he did not, "his memory [was to be] completely obliterated from the fellowship of Christian believers." His books were to be burned, and he and his supporters and followers were to be seized and sent to Rome.

The papal bull came at a busy time for Luther. That fall he wrote what were popularly called the *Three Treatises.* These works, discussed at length in chapter 4, widened the breach between Luther and the church. He, nevertheless, found time to respond to the papal bull in his writing, *On the Detestable Bull of the Antichrist.* At first, Luther liked Leo X. At one point in a letter to the Pope in 1518, Luther expressed his regret that Leo X was the head of the church, noting, "You are worthy of being pope in better days." By 1520 this sentiment changed and Luther was referring to Leo X as the Antichrist. As for the papal bull, when the sixty days transpired, Luther burned it publicly in Wittenberg. When the Pope heard the report of Luther, he excommunicated him and called for his immediate delivery to Rome.

The Diet of Worms

The stage was now set for Luther's showdown with the church. Frederick the Wise again intervened and kept Luther from being sent to Rome. Instead, he was to appear before the Imperial Diet, or congress, at Worms in April 1521. Next to the posting of the *Ninety-Five Theses*, this is the most well-known event in Luther's life. His appearance at Worms has grown to almost mythic proportions. Charles V, the emperor of the Holy Roman Empire, oversaw the Diet. As many historians have noted, the Holy Roman Empire was neither holy, nor Roman, nor much of an empire. It was instead a loose confederacy whose future hung precariously. This was Charles V's debut meeting with the princes and rulers of Germany, and he could not have designed a more difficult challenge. On the one hand, he was staunchly Roman Catholic and heavily indebted to the Roman curia. The papal nuncio, Aleander, was there to ensure that Rome's interests were protected. On the other hand, Charles V ascended to the throne largely through the influence of Frederick the Wise, Luther's protector.

Charles V was in an extremely tenuous position, and so was Luther. Luther arrived to a hero's welcome at Worms, armed for—and anticipating—a debate. He had Scripture on his side, he had Augustine on his side, and he had arguments that would appeal to his fellow Germans on his side. Why, Luther reasoned, abdicate our local, German authority to rule our lands and practice our religion to the Pope in Rome? Instead of engaging in debate, however, Luther underwent an inquisition. When it came time for him to appear before the Diet, he was simply asked two questions: Are these your writings? Do you recant? Luther stood stunned before the assembly. How could they expect him to recant? His writings contained the words of Scripture, the words of the councils, and even the words of the popes. He could not simply dismiss these words. Further, Luther wondered what exactly it was about his writings that troubled Charles V. Luther was more than willing to admit that he was wrong if that could be proven. Rome, however, was beyond wanting to prove Luther wrong; the leaders simply wanted him to go away. Luther requested one day to think things over, and Charles V granted this request.

The next day, April 18, 1521, Luther once again stood before the Diet of Worms. Again he requested a debate, and again he was denied. He then delivered his famous and succinct speech. In full, it reads:

> Since then your serene majesty and your lordships seek a simple answer, I will give it in this manner, not embellished: Unless I am convinced by the testimony of the Scriptures or by clear reason, for I do not trust either in the pope or in councils alone, since it is well known that they have often erred and contradict themselves, I am bound to the Scriptures I have quoted and my conscience is captive to the Word of God. I cannot and I will not retract anything, since it is neither safe nor right to go against conscience. I cannot do otherwise, here I stand. May God help me, Amen.

Some debate exists over whether Luther actually recited the famous three words, "Here I stand." The first printed version of the speech contains the words, with the last part "I cannot do otherwise, here I stand, God help me," in German, while the previous material is in Latin. The three words do not appear in the transcription of the speech. There is no debate, however, concerning the outcome of Luther's address. Refusing to recant, he admitted his guilt, sealing his doom as a heretic. German nobles quickly surrounded him and led him safely from the hall. Charles V released a letter the next day affirming his intention to see that "the notorious heretic" be dealt with immediately. He had, however, to turn his attention to other business matters first. Finally, in May, when it became clear that the German nobles would not hand Luther over to the papal authorities, Charles V placed him under the imperial ban. Luther could be hunted down and killed by anyone—a ruling that he lived under for the rest of his life. Further, anyone harboring Luther would also fall under the same condemnation. Frederick the Wise fully predicted the outcome at Worms. He arranged for Luther to be kidnapped and taken to one of his castles. Frederick also made sure that he did not know where Luther would be taken. For almost a year, Luther assumed a new identity, Junker Jorg. He disguised himself, at one point even dressing as a woman to avoid detection, and hid in Frederick's castle on the high ridge at Wartburg. This one monk stood against the entire church and empire. Luther's activities, once considered by Leo X as the mere ravings of a drunken German, now threatened the church's ascendancy in Germany and across Europe.

The "exile to Patmos," as Luther referred to his seclusion at Frederick's castle, was not without its difficulties. In fact, during these days, Luther faced some of his most intense spiritual struggles, the *anfechtungen* that so characterized his early life. His actions had been unprecedented; he had challenged the church and now stood condemned as her enemy, the enemy of the gospel, and the enemy of Christ himself. During intense spiritual battle at Wartburg, legend has it, Luther hurled an ink well at the wall as the devil appeared to torment him. Though this may likely be myth, undoubtedly Luther was under attack. Writing to a friend, he said, "In this leisurely solitude I am exposed to a thousand devils. It is much easier to fight the devil incarnate—that is, people—than the spirits of iniquity under the heavens." He also added, "Often I fall, but the right hand of the Most High raises me again."

The months at the Wartburg Castle, from May 1521 to March 1522, were actually not very leisurely. During this time, Luther produced an immense literary output, including his translation of the Greek New Testament into German in merely four months. In addition, Luther wrote numerous sermons for the churches of Germany. His theological ideas revolutionized the church service, and the priests needed guidance in their new task: preaching. He also maintained extensive correspondence. In Luther's absence, the church and the university at Wittenberg were threatened by over-zealous supporters. At one point, Luther risked personal harm by returning to Wittenberg for just over a week's time, but retreated quickly to his hiding place.

A few months passed and Luther continued to receive troubling news from Wittenberg. "Junker Jorg's" exiled life came to an end, and Luther returned to Wittenberg. During his absence the political climate had changed drastically. The German princes and Charles V were too busy contending with the approaching Turks to devote resources to tracking down a wayward monk. And Luther still had the support of Frederick the Wise. Luther was still under the ban, as he would be for the remainder of his life, but he was safe in Wittenberg.

By 1521, Luther had accomplished more than most do in many a lifetime. Little doubt that most of the well-known events of his life come from these early years. These years, however full, nevertheless meet their match in the events that fill his later years.

2

THE LATER YEARS

1522–1546

"For you may well believe me, one of his friends: Martin is much greater and more admirable than I could possibly suggest with words. You know how Alcibiades admired Socrates; I admire this man in an entirely different, namely a Christian manner. Every time I think about him, he seems even greater to me!"
Philip Melanchthon

"We are beggars. This is true."
Martin Luther, February 16, 1546

O N MARCH 6, 1522, Luther, still unrecognizable to even his closest friends, returned to Wittenberg. His breach with Rome was both irreparable and final. Now Luther had to oversee the establishment of a new church, and one quite different from its predecessor. Of course, not all of his colleagues and disciples were of the same mind about this challenge. The excesses of Andreas Karlstadt and the "Zwickau prophets," a group of pastors from the nearby town of Zwickau, who originally associated with Luther but moved in more of a fanatical direction, threatened to unravel the precarious coalition of followers. Luther had withstood both pope and emperor, but could he withstand his friends?

The challenges Luther faced in the church comprised only part of the picture, as he also had to contend with the economic and political changes facing the various lands of

Fig. 2.1 Timeline: Later Years

1521–1522	Remains in "exile" at Wartburg Castle from May 1521 to March 1522
1522	Returns to Wittenberg
1523	Composes first hymn, "A New Song Shall Here Be Begun"
1523	Writes *On Temporal Authority*
1524	Publishes first hymnal
1525	Peasants' War occurs
1525	Marries Katherina von Bora on June 13
1525	Writes *Bondage of the Will*
1526	Writes *German Mass*
1527	Plague strikes Wittenberg. Luther house becomes hospital
1527	Composes "A Mighty Fortress Is Our God"
1529	Attends Marburg Colloquy on October 1–4
1529	Writes *Small Catechism*
1530	*Augsburg Confession* is written
1534	Publishes complete German Bible
1537	*Smalcald Articles* are written
1539	Publishes first Wittenberg edition of collected writings
1545	Publishes complete edition of Latin writings with preface containing biographical reflection
1546	Preaches last sermon at Wittenberg on January 17
1546	Dies on February 18 in Eisleben. Buried at Wittenberg

Germany. The German peasants found inspiration in both the life and writings of Martin Luther. As Luther threw off the shackles of the medieval Roman church's oppressive theology, so the peasants sought to rid themselves of the oppressive economic and political structures of the medieval political world. Luther's tenuous and complex relationship with the peasants and their 1525 revolt will be discussed further later. The revolt reveals, however, the far-reaching impact of Luther's action beginning with the posting of the *Ninety-Five Theses* and culminating in his stand before Worms. The entire face of Europe changed; in fact, the modern world and the rise of the nation-state were born. Luther was not far from the center of these events, and he played a role in many of these issues. Hans Holbein, the famous German painter, depicted Luther as the "German Hercules" in 1523. The painting confirms that, in his own day, Luther towered as a larger-than-life figure.

He devoted the majority of his energy, however, to the church. Along with the theological reforms came many far-reaching reforms of church polity and practice. Luther turned his attention to the church service and the relationship between clergy and laity. Here he instituted numerous reforms, including congregational singing, the use of German in addition to Latin, and a newfound emphasis on the sermon. His work in the church was tireless; he devoted boundless energy to preaching, writing, and administrating. And in the midst of all of this activity, he married.

The Marriage of the Monk and the Nun

Among his reforms to church practice, Luther challenged the celibacy of the priesthood and monks. He argued simply that this was not biblical. Luther had advocated this position since the late 1510s. As early as 1521, he published a thorough argument against the vow of celibacy in a work entitled *The Judgment of Martin Luther on Monastic Vows*. He argues here that the monastic vows derive "from a human course," meaning the teaching of the saints and the church which runs contrary to Scripture. He also contends that the vows are against faith because they cause one to focus on a works-oriented approach to salvation. By keeping the vows, Luther believed, priests tried to win God's favor. This stance, of course, gets to the heart of Luther's theology and his emphasis on justification by faith alone. Further, he argues that the vows go against Christian liberty, another crucial theme in his thought. Finally, Luther argues that the vow of celibacy attacks the God-ordained institution of marriage, which he expresses in his own inimitable way:

> These men dare to commit blasphemy . . . where they allege that a man cannot serve God in marriage. What is this but to argue that marriage is perfidy, impiety, and universal apostasy? Does this mean, O Pope, you servant of Satan, that Abraham and all the patriarchs, Zechariah and Elizabeth did not serve God?

He backed up his theoretical view by marrying priests and by assisting nuns in escaping the convents at great personal risk. On one occasion, he assisted twelve nuns in escaping from the Nimbschen convent in Grimma. Luther recruited his friend, Leonard Koppe, a fish merchant in Torgau, to help him. The nuns escaped on a wagon containing barrels used to store herring—undoubtedly not the most pleasant route for travel. Some of the nuns returned to their homes, while others followed Luther to Wittenberg. He assisted all but one of them, Katherina von Bora, in getting married. After a few failed attempts at matchmaking, it became obvious to most observers, except of course to Luther, that perhaps she and

2.2 The title page of Luther's response to the Louvain Catholic theologians contains Albrecht Durer's woodcut of Samson slaying a lion. The publisher made a clever wordplay between the German spelling of Louvain and the word for lion. The meaning is clear: As Samson slays the lion, Luther slays the Catholic theologians.

the reformer should marry. Luther expressed his reluctance; he did not mind life under the ban, but he hesitated to place a wife and potential family in harm's way. His reluctance did not last long, however. Katherina and Martin's courtship was brief, the engagement briefer still. He did not believe in long engagements: "By delay Hannibal lost Rome, by delay Esau forfeited his birthright. Christ said, 'You shall seek me, and ye shall not find.' Scripture, experience and all creation testify that the gifts of God must be taken on the wing."

Luther personalized his endorsement of a married clergy by marrying Katherina von Bora on June 13, 1525. In doing so, he said, "I hope all the angels will laugh and the devils will weep." Luther offered many reasons for his marriage. He owed his parents grandchildren, he reasoned, and he enjoyed upsetting the papists. In inviting a friend to attend their wedding, Luther wrote, "The rumor of my marriage is correct. I cannot deny my father the hope of progeny, and I had to confirm my teaching at a time when many are so timid." But he did not marry for love. Over time, however, even this gruff, confirmed bachelor was won over. He confesses, "I would not exchange my Katie for Paris or all of France, for Venice or all of Italy, for God has given her to me and has given me to her." At one point in the "Table Talk" he writes, "There is no sweeter union than that in a good marriage." The union between Martin and Katie grew stronger over the years and through the trials they faced together. Luther often expressed his absolute dependence on Katie, whom he affectionately referred to as "my rib."

A Perfect School for Character

Marrying Katie presented Luther with a new challenge. What should a parsonage look like? There were no models, no precedents, so the Luthers pioneered new ground in making one. Luther referred to the home "as a perfect school for character." His "school" grew to six children of their own, and eventually four orphans of relatives who lost their lives in the plague. Many other children spent days and nights in the Luther home. To accommodate such a crowd, they needed a large house, and Frederick the Wise anticipated this by generously giving the "Black Cloister" to the Luthers as a wedding present. The same monastery that was home to Luther the monk since 1509 now served the home for the married pastor and as the first parsonage in the modern age. The house was quite large, with ample living quarters on one side and large and small lecture rooms on the other. This house, now referred to as the *Lutherhalle,* stands as a museum to its famous resident and the Reformation that he spawned.

Luther's home, with its frequent visitors, left his family open to public view. There is ample public record of Luther's activities, which reveal Luther as a colorful historical figure. And while some public figures disappoint in their personal lives, this is not the case with Luther. In fact, when we look at his private life, the picture that emerges may be even more endearing than the public portrait. One of the most tender moments for the Luther family came at the death of his thirteen-year-old daughter, Magdelena, on September 20, 1542, after suffering a severe, yet swift-moving illness. The Luthers had lost one child already, Elizabeth, who died at just seven months. Magdelena, or "Little Lena," as Luther called her, was the apple of his eye. Just before she died, Luther prayed, "I love Magdelena dearly. But if it is your will, dear God, to take her away, I shall be happy to know that she is with you." He then turned to his daughter and gently asked, "My little Magdelena, my little daughter, would you like to stay here with me, with your father? Yet, you would also gladly go to your Father beyond?" "Yes, dear father," she answered, "it is as God wills." Luther then said to her, "You dear daughter. The spirit is strong, but the flesh is weak. If her flesh is so strong, what then must her spirit be."

Luther also showed a deep respect for his wife Katie as seen in discussions recorded in the "Table Talk." He considered Katie his equal and engaged her in many theological discussions, which his colleagues and students simply observed.

In addition to her sharp mind, Katie also tirelessly managed an ever-growing family, as well as the demands of the Black Cloister and other family properties. Over the years, both Frederick the Wise, the Elector of Saxony, and his nephew and successor, John Frederick, gave the Luthers many properties and gifts. Luther was generous in giving away gifts and monies without hesitation, and even his and Katie's wedding gifts could be passed along to someone in need. Katie realized quickly that if she wanted to keep a particular item, she needed to hide it.

Luther left a sizable estate after his death, lending a certain irony to his parents' concerns after he abandoned a more lucrative career in the law. And it was Katie who managed the money and the properties. One such property was the former Brisger home in Wittenberg, which was at the time a *brauhaus,* or brewery. This welcomed asset provided the refreshment for the table talks. On several occasions in writing to his wife during his travels, Luther mentioned how he longed to be home and to have his Katie's brew. In addition, Luther purchased a farm in Zulsdorf for his wife that she had visited as a child and which belonged to Katie's brother. This farm provided a perfect retreat for the Luthers from life at Wittenberg. Also, they owned three gardens and a fish pond, as well as various livestock. Between the properties, the farms, entertaining, church work, lecturing, writing, and traveling, the Luther family remained extremely busy. Luther confesses on more than one occasion that it was Katie who held all of these activities together.

The German Bible

Returning to the public Luther, after his marriage in 1525, he continued to apply his energies to the church. That fall he wrote his theological masterpiece, *The Bondage of the Will.*

This work, a response to Erasmus' criticism on Luther's views on such doctrines as original sin, the will, and sovereignty, remains one of the essential texts from church history that grapples with the age-old controversy orbiting these issues. Numerous other projects also received his attention, including the German Bible translation. Begun during his exile at the Wartburg, the German Bible occupied Luther's thoughts throughout most of his life. He finished the New Testament in 1522. When he returned to Wittenberg, he made continual revisions and set up a translation committee for the Old Testament. Translating large portions himself, overseeing the work of the translation committee, and approving essentially each and every word resulted in the publication of the very first translation of the entire German Bible in 1534.

More than five hundred woodcuts by Lucas Cranach the Elder and the Younger, as well as by others, illustrated the first complete edition of the Bible. These illustrations, typical of Renaissance art, used sixteenth-century dress and settings to illustrate biblical characters and events. Not a few of them vilified the Pope and other Roman church officials and practices. Once the Bible was published, Luther and his committee did not stop their work, but rather continued to revise the text. In fact, Luther continued meeting with the committee as late as the last year before his death. The German Bible reflects his commitment to the Reformation principle of *sola Scriptura*; it stands as a legacy of his desire to recapture the centrality of the Word for the church. To this day, Luther's translation is widely used in his native land. In fact, many have pointed out that Luther's word choices from the range of German dialects and his choice of syntax profoundly impacted the development of modern German grammar.

The Bible was not the only book he translated. As a child he loved to hear Aesop's Fables. As an adult, he loved to read them to children. His debt to Aesop's Fables can be seen in his frequent application of the animal characters to his opponents in the Roman Church. As one might surmise, the jackass was clearly a personal favorite. He so liked these tales that he made his own German translation of them, which also long outlived its translator. Luther's joy in teaching children, as well as his travels, impressed upon him the need to teach the church's beliefs to the next generation. During these travels, he became acutely aware of the lack of theological understanding and ability among clergy and laity alike. In 1529 he produced both the *Large* and *Small Catechism* to remedy this urgent deficiency, the former being for the clergy, the latter for the children. These works testify that Luther was more than a visionary, as he was also committed to the ordinary tasks required to move the church beyond its incubation on to maturity. And it also demonstrates that he recognized the importance of training the next generation in the faith.

Luther's Impact

Luther's work in his later years extended beyond the borders of Germany to greater Europe and beyond. His writings had a profound influence on a young student at Paris' University of Montaigu in the 1520s. The theological faculty there was tasked with evaluating Luther's debate with Eck in 1519, not an easy task. Luther clearly put forth the better ideas, yet to side with him would mean to condone a heretic. Eventually, the faculty declared Eck the winner. In the process, however, the ideas of Luther were introduced to that young student, John Calvin. Calvin went on to reach similar conclusions. While Calvin ended up agreeing with Luther, he came to these conclusions independently. Some Calvin scholars see this early connection to Luther as quite influential. The two reformers never met, although they corresponded frequently and read each other's works. Luther's influence may also be seen in the reforms at Zurich through Ulrich Zwingli's work. Zwingli and Luther did meet at the Marburg Colloquy in 1529. This event, discussed at length later, proved pivotal not only for the theological landscape, but also for the political one. Phillip of Hesse, who convened the colloquy, or meeting, wanted a unified front among the various reform parties. His desire, however, did not reach fruition since Luther and Zwingli disagreed over the nature of the Lord's Supper.

As Luther left Marburg and entered the decade of the 1530s, he devoted himself to writing. By 1537, Luther turned from writer to editor, as he shepherded through the press the first of what would be many printings of his collected writings in German. A large portion of these writings were his sermons and commentaries. Primarily, these writings consist of student notes taken as he lectured and preached. Perhaps his most well-known commentaries are on the books of Galatians and Romans. These were the books that first led Luther to great spiritual struggles after studying them. They also eventually led Luther to resolve those struggles. Luther once referred to Paul's Epistle to the Galatians as "my Katherina Von Bora, I am betrothed to it"—a compliment extended both to Galatians and to Katie. In his preface, he first admits that he can hardly believe how verbose he was in his lectures, then adds that what he found in Galatians is central to his theological understanding: "The one doctrine which I have supremely at heart, is that of faith in Christ, from whom, through whom, and unto whom all my theological thinking flows back and forth day and night."

His commentary on Galatians has made a profound impact on many. John Bunyan, the Puritan author of *Pilgrim's Progress,* once remarked, "I do prefer this book of Martin Luther upon the Galatians, excepting the Holy Bible, before all books that ever I have seen, as most fit for a wounded conscience." This commentary also influenced Charles Wesley. Wesley was reading the preface to two other men, causing one of them, William Holland, to record "my heart was so filled with peace and love, that I burst into tears." In his journal Wesley records the impact it had on him personally.

2.3 A portrait of Luther in 1546, just before his death.

He recalls that after the group dispersed, "I spent some hours that evening in private with Martin Luther, who was greatly blessed to me." Four days later, Wesley was converted. Three days later, his famous brother, John Wesley, was similarly impacted by Luther's preface to the commentary on Romans. He stopped along Aldersgate Street to eavesdrop on a Moravian meeting. Listening to someone reading from the preface, he later recorded in his journal, he felt his heart "strangely warmed." Both the commentary on Galatians and on Romans continue to affect readers to this day.

Again, these commentaries were originally lectures, and there were plenty of students from among whom Luther could choose his note takers. In the years 1541–1545 alone, 2,928 students passed through the University of Wittenberg and heard Luther lecture at the Black Cloister. One in every ten students was foreign born, which means Luther influenced a virtual army of pastors and trained leaders not only in Germany, but around the world. One such student, an Italian named Giordano Bruno, memorialized Luther and Wittenberg in the following poem:

> They came from all peoples and every land
> Where culture and Order were in demand:
> They came from Italy, France, and Spain;
> The Poles, the Slavs, from Magyar's plain;
> The British, Scotch, and Portugese,
> The Scandinavians from Nordic Seas,
> Yes, even from the Balkan state,
> From farthest Caucasus they congregate.
> From morn to eve, from noon to night,
> Welding the new day's circle tight.

Many of these students faced intense religious persecution, and some died as martyrs after returning to their homelands. Giordano Bruno was imprisoned during the Inquisition and burned at the stake for his beliefs.

Luther's Inner Circle

Luther enjoyed the company of his colleagues at Wittenberg in educating students. He and his elder colleague, Andreas Karlstadt, experienced a rocky relationship, however. Karlstadt began the relationship as a strong ally. When he took drastic reform measures, like smashing statues and breaking stained glass windows, as well as expressing Anabaptist views, Luther rebuked his elder. Karlstadt, in turn, attacked Luther, even denouncing him publicly. During July 1525, Karlstadt, literally running for his life, sought refuge with Luther. Luther took him in, a tribute to the Protestant reformer's character. Johannes Bugenhagen, another colleague, first joined Luther's cause in 1520 when he read *The Babylonian Captivity of the Church*. He became a colleague on the faculty with Luther at Wittenberg the next year. He and Luther shared many of the preaching duties in the Castle Church. Additionally, Bugenhagen played a key role on the committee translating the Old Testament. Another close friend, though not a colleague at the university, was George Spalatin. He studied law with Luther at Erfurt. Their paths crossed again as Spalatin, both a lawyer and a priest, served as the personal secretary to Frederick the Wise, the Elector of Saxony. As one can well imagine, Spalatin came to Luther's aid on more than one occasion. Another friend and fellow pastor at Wittenberg, Justas Jonas, supported Luther faithfully, spent many hours at his table, and shared Luther's passion for hymn writing. Jonas also preached Luther's funeral sermon at Wittenberg in 1546.

Among his friends and colleagues, however, Philip Melancthon stands as the most well known. Melanchthon excelled in the languages, writing a Greek grammar in his twentieth year. He arrived in Wittenberg in 1518, in time to witness Luther's debates first with Cajetan, then with Eck. When Melancthon came to Wittenberg to teach the biblical languages, Luther won him over to theology. Quite popular as a lecturer, "his classroom is jammed with students," Luther observed. Melanchthon grew in prominence at virtually the same pace with Luther. During Luther's exile at the Wartburg Castle, Melanchthon published the *Loci Communes,* Common Places, a systematic theology emphasizing Luther's new theological discoveries. They enjoyed a lifetime friendship, although they were quite different personalities. Luther once remarked that Melancthon stabbed with pins and needles, while he himself stabbed with a heavy spear. Melancthon was much quieter and more gentle, a chemistry that sometimes proved efficient and at other times proved quite frustrating to Luther.

Melanchthon, who was not under the ban, went to the Diet at Augsburg in 1530 to represent Luther's view. Luther kept in close contact through correspondence of the unfolding events. Charles V had called the Diet in the hope of unifying the German princes and rulers in order to stand against the encroaching "Turks" or Muslims. He came to seek theological unity. The German princes, however, would not move from Luther's position. They tasked Melanchthon with writing the final draft of the *Augsburg Confession,* a text which, although preferring certain points to be stated more strongly, Luther fully approved. There is some dispute over Melanchthon's changing the language at the last moment on certain points, but the text remains a statement of Luther's and Lutheran doctrine. The *Smalcald Articles,* 1537, represent Luther's own theological confession. These two texts, along with Luther's *Large* and *Small Catechisms,* as well as several other documents, comprise *The Book of Concord,* 1578, the doctrinal confession of the Lutheran church. Both the *Smalcald Articles* and the *Catechisms* summarize Luther's theology and serve as his confessional legacy to the church that bears his name.

Legs of Iron, Feet of Clay

Several illnesses plagued Luther's later years. He often attributed his sickness to the years of torture that he subjected his body to while in the monastery. Rarely, however, did he let his illnesses slow down his work. He kept up his prodigious writing, as well as his travels to various churches. Luther was in constant demand, both to preach and to lend his expertise in administrative matters. Several times, parties in a dispute relied on him to mediate a resolution. This aspect of Luther's legacy, lesser known to us today, nevertheless reveals that he committed his life not just to starting a new church, but also to seeing it grow. His commitment extended over the long haul and stands as an extraordinary example of one who found the boldness to stand at the crucial moments and the stamina to keep at the ordinary tasks.

One of Luther's legacies that does not shine so brightly concerns his attitude toward the Jews. This largely stems from his 1543 work entitled *On the Jews and Their Lies*. The text, critics say, reveals Luther's anti-Semitism and provides inspiration for those who committed the horrific atrocities against Jews during the Holocaust. Many scholars claim that Luther's criticism of the Jews was not racial, but rather religious. In other words, Luther attacked Jews as vehemently as he attacked Muslims or the papists. While this view serves to mitigate Luther's comments, his harsh statements leave an unfortunate legacy. They serve to remind us that while Luther, indeed, had legs of iron, he, nevertheless, had feet of clay.

In 1545, the first volumes of the Latin edition of his works, known as the Wittenberg Edition, began to appear. By 1546, Luther writes to a fellow pastor that he feels as "one who is old, worn-out, sluggish, tired, cold, and now even one-eyed, as one who feels himself long dead and deserving—so it seems to me—that a rest be granted him." That same day, January 18, 1546, he preached his last sermon at Wittenberg. Undoubtedly intending to take the rest he so craved, Luther was, instead, called to Eisleben, the town of his birth, to settle a dispute. Along the way, Luther and his party encountered treacherous weather, and Luther became gravely ill. He arrived finally in Eisleben to a hero's welcome, escorted into the town by an honor guard of no fewer than 113 soldiers on horses. After recovering from his illness, he managed to have the disputing parties work out a resolution, and he also preached four sermons.

As Luther was about to leave the town, however, his illness recurred, preventing him from returning home. Since leaving Wittenberg, he corresponded with Katie, who had heard rumors that he either was on his deathbed or that he had drowned in a flooding river. Luther kept assuring his wife that she need not worry as he had a protector, one who "lies in a manger and clings to a virgin's breast, and yet one who is at the same time seated at the right hand of God the Father Almighty. Therefore, be satisfied." That was on February 7. By February 16, with the illness growing worse, Luther knew he was about to die. He asked for some paper and wrote the following:

> Nobody can understand Virgil in his Bucolics, unless he has been a shepherd for five years. Nobody can understand Virgil in his Georgics, unless he has been a plowman for five years. Nobody can understand Cicero in his Epistles, unless he has lived for twenty-five years in a large

empire. Let no one think that he has sufficiently grasped the Holy Scriptures, unless he has governed the churches for a hundred years for prophets like Elijah and Elisha, John the Baptist, Christ, and the apostles. Don't venture on this divine Aeneid, but rather bend low in reverence before its footprints. We are beggars! That is true.

Two days later, within view of the baptismal font where he was christened, Martin Luther died. His struggles had finally been resolved. The God, who at one time struck terror to his very soul by just the mere thought of him, was now viewed as welcoming him with arms wide open. Those gathered by Luther's deathbed recorded his final words. Just before he died, he prayed, "I thank you God and Father of our Lord Jesus Christ, that you have revealed your dear son to me, in whom I have believed, and whom I have preached, confessed, and trusted." Then he offered his last "sermon," which consisted of reciting John 3:16 and Psalm 68:20. The latter reads: "Our God is a God of salvation; and to God, the Lord, belongs escape from death."

The news of Luther's death spread quickly. When Melanchthon, lecturing at the university, heard the news, he stopped teaching and said, "It was not human brilliance that discovered the doctrine of the forgiveness of sin and of faith in the Son of God, but God who raised him up before our very eyes, who has revealed these truths through him. Let us hold dear the memory of this man and the doctrine in the very manner in which he delivered it to us." Luther's body was returned to Wittenberg, where he lies buried in the Castle Church.

Luther's legacy includes the church that bears his name, as well as all who call themselves Protestants. Many of the doctrines and practices that define the various Protestant traditions trace their roots to Martin Luther. In addition, he left behind such a breadth of writings that the attempt to produce a complete edition of all of his works, which began in 1883, continues to this day. The *Weimar Ausgabe,* or edition, already numbers one hundred volumes, and is still growing. The authoritative English edition of his works, a translation of selections from this edition, simply known as *Luther's Works,* consists of fifty-six volumes. These works include treatises, sermons, commentaries, letters, and many pamphlets or smaller writings. Luther often expressed his own astonishment at what God accomplished through his life. He also said, "I'd rather that all my books would disappear and the Holy Scriptures alone would be read." He even added, "Who will read them?" Luther's writings have found readers, and on many occasions those readers were helped to understand Scripture better through his writings.

Evaluating Luther

At one point during his exile at the Wartburg Castle in the spring of 1523, Luther, needing a change of scenery from his refuge, stopped at a nearby inn. He was sitting alone, disguised as a knight, at a table reading a Hebrew copy of the Psalter. Two Swiss students entered and Luther could not resist inviting them to join him at his table. As the conversation unfolded, the subject of Martin Luther surfaced. "Dear Sir," the students inquired of this seeming German Knight, "are you able to tell us whether Martin Luther is now at Wittenberg, or where he might be?" Luther, only answering the first part, assured them, "I know for certain that right now Luther is not at Wittenberg." Then he inquired of them, "Good fellows, what opinion do the people of Switzerland have of Luther?" They replied, "My lord, as everywhere else, the opinions vary. There are some who cannot praise him sufficiently, thanking God that through him he has revealed the truth and brought to light the errors; but some, especially the clergy, condemn him as a troublesome heretic." Luther responded, "Unless I am mistaken, they are papists."

As the conversation continued, the students' suspicions grew about this knowledgeable knight. When they saw his Hebrew Psalter, those suspicions grew greater. It was not until after "Junker Jorg" had left, however, that the innkeeper informed them that they were eating with the outlaw himself. Their conversation with Luther, which they later recorded, reveals a certain irony. Luther began his quest to resolve his spiritual struggles embraced by the church and, in his mind, abandoned by God. He resolved his struggles embraced by God and abandoned by the church. Although that would be more than enough for Luther, he was also embraced by those thankful to God for using this monk to recover the treasure of the gospel. This, of course, was not only true in his own day, but continues five centuries later.

A Note on the Sources

Biographies of Luther, of which there are many, will be discussed in the conclusion. Primary sources concerning biographical issues and details may be found in *Luther's Works, Volumes 48–50: Letters I, II, and III* (1963), edited by Gottfried G. Krodel. Also helpful is the material in *Luther's Works, Volume 54: Table Talk* (1967), edited by Theodore G. Tappert. Oskar Thulin's *A Life of Luther* (1966) offers a thorough chronological account with extensive quotes from primary sources, including Luther's writings and those of contemporary friends and foes.

PART TWO

LUTHER, THE REFORMER

THIS SECTION EXPLORES those writings which led directly to the Reformation and continue to impact Protestant theology today. We begin with an overview of Luther's theology. Luther never wrote a systematic theology, yet as his works unfold, several themes and key emphases emerge. This chapter sets these themes out in a systematic fashion to provide the big picture of his thought. Next comes a treatment of the *Three Treatises*, a series of works written during the crucial fall months of 1520. Here Luther moves far beyond the *Ninety-Five Theses* in his critique of Rome. His theological magnum opus, *The Bondage of the Will*, becomes the focus of the next chapter. Here his thoughts on the challenging issue of God's sovereignty and the human will unfold before us.

It may come as a surprise to some that the issue that blocked the reformers in Germany, Luther and his associates, from uniting with the reformers in the Swiss Confederacy, Zwingli and his followers, concerned the Lord's Supper. Chapter 6 examines this issue to understand why it came to be such a crucial factor. Finally, even if unintended, Luther's theological reformation inspired a virtual social revolution.

Responding to the issues swirling around him, Luther developed intriguing ideas related to ethics and the Christian's role and duty in this world. All of these works profoundly impacted the first generation that read them. They are not simply timely texts, however. They continue to reward readers and stand among the great classics of the Christian faith.

3

THE MEAT OF THE NUT

Understanding Luther's Theology

"It's very hard for a man to believe that God is gracious to him.
The human heart can't grasp this."
Martin Luther, 1531

A S MENTIONED EARLIER, Luther never wrote a systematic theology. His theology developed in the
trenches, as it were, as he was thrust into conflicts and
engaged in the controversies of his day. Certainly, a system
revealing distinct themes and taking on a structure emerges
from his work, though not all at one time, nor in one place.
But to navigate the labyrinthine contours of Luther's theology without a structure or guide is like exploring a vast cave
system without a map. Eventually you will most likely make
it out, and you will probably even enjoy the sites along the
way, but a map would certainly have eased the journey. As
we begin to explore Luther as a reformer and tackle his ideas
and writings, it may be helpful first to look at "a map," or
overview of his theology.

69

In the spring of 1509, Luther, settled in Wittenberg and beginning his career as a professor of theology and Bible, wrote a letter to Johann Braun, a priest at Eisenach whom he greatly admired. In the letter, Luther expresses his goal for his teaching and writing, noting that fundamentally he wanted to pursue a theology "that would penetrate to the meat of the nut, to the very core of the wheat grain, to the marrow of the bone." It would be some time before Luther would arrive there, yet his unique methodology given his historical context clearly evidences itself in these words. Not content with his colleagues' approach, which largely consisted of rehearsing the tradition's teaching in an encyclopedic fashion, Luther longed to go deeper, to get to the heart of the matter, to get at the meat of the nut. This radical starting point led to a radical way of thinking that quickly distinguished Luther from his peers. And, tracing the path of these thoughts leads us to that map of his theology. Our journey begins with what may well be Luther's most significant theological breakthrough, the theology of the cross.

Sinners at the Root

John Calvin, Luther's fellow reformer from Geneva, begins his monumental work of theology, *The Institutes of the Christian Religion,* with a dilemma. Do we look to God to understand humanity? Or, do we look to humanity to understand God? Calvin did both; Luther tried looking to God. But, the closer he looked, the more terrified he became. Little wonder then, that as he began earnestly studying and teaching theology, Luther felt much more comfortable looking to humanity and, more specifically, to himself. What he found, however, left him unsettled. Nevertheless, as we know to be true, one has little appreciation for the glorious work of redemption without first coming face to face with the ugly realities of sin. So it is with Luther; on his road to redemption from his struggles, he had to stop at what surely must have seemed a detour and grapple with sin.

Luther comes to understand sin in a radically different way than both medieval and early sixteenth-century notions of sin. As we saw earlier, he understood sin not just as the sins that one commits, but as one's very nature; we are sinners at the "root." This new perspective provides Luther's already sensitive conscience with even more fodder and casts him further into his *anfechtungen,* or spiritual struggles. Years later, reflecting back on this time, Luther wrote, "I didn't learn my theology all at once, I had to ponder over it even more deeply, and my spiritual trials were of help to me in this." His contemporaries, however, preferred to speak of sins, not sin. Luther came to the understanding that his problem was much deeper than what he did, for it encompassed who he was. To focus on sins simply quantified it, which also led to quantifying grace. This proposition further led to the penitential system, reducing grace to the level of canceling out the demerits of sins. By Luther's day this view had developed into a complex system. The belief emerged in the Catholic church that the saints had accumulated more grace than they needed, which then served much like a treasury. Those who did not live such saintly lives and needed grace could pray to the saints for their extra grace.

If, however, our problem is deeper than simply the sins we commit, then this system of credits and debits does not go far enough. Undoubtedly, Luther's understanding of sin as much more than a problem of sins explains his dissatisfaction with the prescriptions of medieval theology. It also becomes clearer to us why he struggled so intensely and even raged against God. Given the climate of his day, he knew of no such remedy for his soul. This struggle led him to look elsewhere than the theologians of the Middle Ages.

It drove him straight to the Bible, and from there he was pointed to the cross.

The Theology of the Cross

Luther's spiritual crises met resolution when he finally reached the meat of the nut, the theology of the cross. Luther's first writing on the subject comes at the end of the *Ninety-Five Theses*. There he expresses, "Away, then, with all those prophets who say to the people of Christ, 'Peace, peace,' and there is no peace! Blessed be all those prophets who say to the people of Christ, 'Cross, cross,' and there is no cross!" Luther's poetic contrast of peace and the cross, *Pax* and *Crux* in Latin, criticizes the indulgence preachers and indulgence sale for offering glory without suffering, or peace without addressing the horrors of sin. This "peace" is in fact false, and, consequently, leaves one without peace. One who preaches the cross, however, acknowledges the horror of sin.

Luther developed this nascent idea further in another set of theses, or arguments, prepared for a debate at Heidelberg in 1518. In the *Heidelberg Disputation,* he writes, "He deserves to be called a theologian, however, who comprehends the visible and manifest things of God seen through suffering and the cross. A theologian of glory calls evil good and good evil. A theologian of the cross calls the thing what it actually is." These short statements reveal volumes concerning Luther's theology.

First, he contrasts the theology of glory with the theology of the cross. The theology of glory represents two interrelated but distinct elements. First, it focuses on human ability. In order to grasp this aspect fully we need to understand some elements of medieval theology. From the days of Thomas Aquinas, 1225–1274, the theological consensus was that human nature was not entirely fallen. This belief

72

especially concerned the use of reason, but also addressed human ability to achieve righteousness. This view held that humanity cooperates with the grace of God in the act of salvation, as well as the ongoing act of sanctification. Additionally, the capability to use reason correctly implies that God may be known through reason and philosophical speculation. This concept had great appeal to the later medieval theologians, as well as Luther's contemporaries. This method of theology is the second element in Luther's designation of the theology of glory.

The theology of the cross dismantles both elements of the theology of glory. We'll deal with Luther's method of theology first. Before we do, however, we need to revisit the medieval period. Theologians used two contrasting terms to distinguish between how God may be known—the "hidden God" and the "revealed God." To Luther, the "hidden God," or as in Latin the *Deus absconditus*, refers to the invisible God, the unknowable God who transcends human understanding. The revealed God, *Deus revelatus*, refers to God as he has revealed himself and as he may be known. Luther calls this the theology of the cross because it is precisely on the cross that God reveals himself. This dynamic of the hidden and revealed God reflects, according to Luther, the way in which God relates to his people.

This dynamic is first seen in the book of Exodus. On the one hand, the Exodus text continually confronts one with the inaccessibility of God. Only Moses can meet with God, and even then he can only see the hind parts of the Creator as he passes by (Ex. 33). On the other, the text teaches that God offers access to himself by telling Moses that on the mercy seat, "There . . . I will meet with you" (Ex. 25:22). Curiously, the same word used in the Greek translation of the Old Testament, or the Septuagint, is the same as the one used in Romans 3:25, typically translated as propitiation, or atoning sacrifice. In other words, linking the Romans and Exodus passages together, Christ is our mercy seat, and it is in Christ, on the cross, where we meet God. As Luther exclaims, "God wants to be heard through the Propitiator, and so he'll listen to nobody except through Christ. . . . Those who don't seek God or the Lord in Christ, won't find him."

When we do meet Christ on the cross, Luther argues, this should jar us to a halt. Christ is God of the universe, dying on the cross, bearing our shame, and enduring our penalty for sin. The cross is not where Christ should be. Luther adds this is the only place where we deserve to be. Yet, this is where we find Christ, and where we meet God. As Luther writes, "Now it is not sufficient for anyone, and it does him no good to recognize God in his glory and majesty, unless he recognizes him in the humility and shame of the cross. . . . For this reason true theology and recognition of God are in the crucified Christ." "God can be found," he adds, "only in suffering and the cross."

With this understanding of the theology of the cross in place, we can now turn to the first element of the theology of glory, namely human ability to achieve righteousness. In light of Christ on the cross, any trust in human ability becomes sheer folly. Any attempt to reach God through philosophical speculation also becomes futile. As Luther, reflecting on 1 Corinthians 1, notes, through the foolishness of the cross, "God destroys the wisdom of the wise." The theology of glory celebrates works and what humanity can do; the theology of the cross celebrates Christ and what he alone can accomplish. The theology of the cross also deals a crushing blow to a life that is consumed by the self. To see this aspect of Luther's thought, we need to return to his understanding of sin.

As mentioned earlier, the Latin word *radix,* root, summarizes Luther's distinct understanding of sin. We could add another Latin word, *incurvitas,* "curved in." This word conveys the image of selfishness as the self is curved inward. The irony of this tendency is that what seems to promote the self actually leads to destroy the self; our self-interest brings about our self-destruction. Luther explains the implication of this as he makes the following comment on Paul's teaching of the sinful flesh in Romans 8:

> It enjoys only itself and uses everyone else, even God; it seeks itself and its own interests in everything: it brings it about that man is finally and ultimately concerned only for himself. This is the idolatry that determines all he does, feels, undertakes, thinks, and speaks. Good is only what is good for him and bad only what is bad for him.

The theology of the cross stands against this perspective of the self. As historian Mark Noll has observed, the cross declares "God's everlasting 'no' " to the idolatry of the self. The theology of glory exalts the self and actually advances the curve inward. The theology of the cross forces one to look outward, away from the self, and upon seeing Christ, to realize its true and desperate need. This truth reminds us of another irony, that the one who loses his or her life for Christ's sake finds it (Matt. 10:39).

The theology of the cross not only realizes that Christ alone, through his work on the cross, brings about reconciliation with God, but also serves as the undergirding for Luther's approach to—and method of—theology. In a "Table Talk" selection from 1532, Luther, discussing the "hidden" and "revealed" God, observes, "He is visible through his Word and work. Apart from his Word and work, no one should look for him. These theologians [of glory] have wished to apprehend God through speculations and have paid no attention to the Word." Luther then instructs his younger disciples gathered around his table: "I recommend that speculation be laid aside, and I should like to have this rule adhered to after my death." On another occasion, he encouraged those who would be pastors: "This one thing preach, the wisdom of the cross."

The Reformation *Solas*

At virtually the same time Luther was working out his theology of the cross, he was also developing the *solas* (or *solae*) of the Reformation. The Latin word *sola* simply means alone. When Luther couples it with the following series of words he, once again, distinguishes himself from his contemporaries. First Luther asserted *sola Scriptura,* Scripture alone, emphasizing that Scripture alone is the church's authority. Next Luther spoke of *sola fide* and *sola gratia,* stressing that salvation is by grace alone, through faith alone. Finally, Luther posited *solus Christus,* Christ alone, capturing Paul's words proclaiming only one mediator between God and humanity (1 Tim. 2:5). These doctrines encompass the richness of Reformation theology and its legacy to the church. They signal a return to the primacy of Scripture and its teaching concerning God, humanity, and salvation. And, they continue to be the hallmark of Protestant theology, expressing the heart of an orthodox theology.

These doctrines also provide a helpful window through which we can view Luther's writings. As mentioned in

Fig. 3.1 The Reformation *Solas*

Sola Scriptura	Scripture alone
Sola fide	Faith alone
Sola gratia	Grace alone
Solus Christus	Christ alone
Soli Deo gloria	To the glory of God alone

previous chapters, Luther devoted considerable energy to the translation and publication of the German Bible, a testimony to his commitment to *sola Scriptura*. His arrival at this doctrine came in the aftermath of the debates with Cajetan and Eck. Prior to these debates, Luther lectured on Scripture, including lectures on Psalms, Romans, Galatians, and Hebrews. And, prior to these debates, the biblical text played a prominent role in medieval theology. Yet, as he disputed with Rome, the distinctions between Luther's use of the text and the Roman church's use became patently obvious. The Roman approach became canon law, or church law, through the Catholic response to Luther at the Council of Trent, 1545–1563.

In some ways, Trent and its decreetals and articles signaled a victory for Luther as the council outlawed indulgence sellers and instituted strict reforms of church polity and practice. Essentially, however, the Council of Trent offered the church's rebuke of Luther and those who followed his heretical teachings. Justification by faith received prominent attention, but so did his doctrine of Scripture. On this latter topic, Trent declared that the phrase "Scripture and Tradition" best captures the basis for the church's authority. It further declared that the Vulgate, the translation of the Bible into Latin, would be the official text for theological dispute.

This decree directly challenged Luther's *sola Scriptura* principle. As one reads through Trent, it might be better to view the "and" in "Scripture *and* Tradition" as "Scripture *as it is interpreted through the* Tradition," emphasizing the church's authority and guardianship over the text. This addition expresses precisely Luther's problem with the Roman church. For Luther, the authority is Scripture alone. We need to be clear as to what Luther fully intends by the doctrine. He does not mean that everyone can understand and interpret it without help. He views the church, especially the church's activity of preaching the Word, as God's intended means to enable one to better understand Scripture, and he does not disavow tradition, as some might conclude from the *sola Scriptura* principle. Rather, the history of interpretation of texts can be an important safeguard for testing our interpretations. Again, *sola Scriptura* concerns the authority question. It reminds us that we submit to the text; it does not submit to us. As Luther's dying words attest, we bow before Scripture.

Sola Scriptura also means that the Bible stands as the only sure and necessary guide for life and godliness. Luther not only stated this principle, he lived it, as he made a commitment to turn to the Scriptures on a daily basis. He was so faithful to the reading of the Bible that he read through the entire Bible two times annually. He once remarked, "If you picture the Bible to be a mighty tree and every word a little branch, I have shaken every one of those branches because I wanted to know what it was and what it meant."

Luther, as he did with *sola Scriptura,* also expressed his understanding of justification by faith alone, *sola fide,* early on. In a sermon from 1519, entitled "Two Kinds of Righteousness," Luther explains, "Through faith in Christ, therefore, Christ's righteousness becomes our righteousness and all that he has becomes ours; rather he himself becomes ours." Luther clearly understood that the type of righteousness, or in fact the only righteousness, that God desired was something that was foreign to us. As we saw in chapter 1, this "alien righteousness," as Luther calls it, cannot come from within us. He writes in the preface to his Galatians commentary that "we are redeemed from sin, death, and the devil, and made partakers of eternal life, not by ourselves and certainly not by our works, which are less than ourselves, but by the help of another, the only-begotten son of God, Jesus Christ." He also notes later in the commentary, in the righteousness of

Christ, "we work nothing, and we render nothing unto God, but only we receive and suffer another to work in us, that is to say God." For Luther, as we saw in chapter 1 in recalling his conversion, this righteousness is described best as "passive righteousness," emphasizing that Christ works within us.

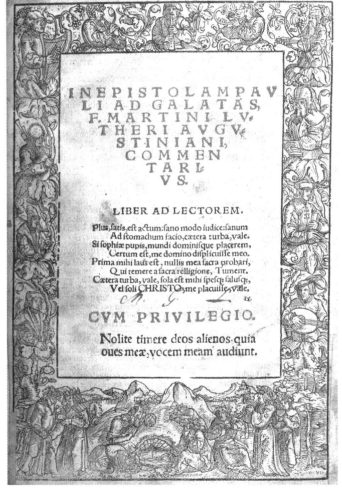

3.2 The title page of Martin Luther's *Commentary on Galatians*, which consisted mainly of his lectures and was published in 1519 while he was still an Augustinian monk.

Elsewhere, in the *Heidelberg Disputation,* Luther clearly distinguishes the doctrine of justification by faith alone from the works-oriented approach of his contemporaries. Again, as with *sola Scriptura,* we need to be careful how we understand Luther on this point. Perhaps foreseeing potential misinterpretation, Luther writes that he wishes to "have the words 'without works' understood in the following manner: Not that the righteous person does nothing, but that his works do not make him righteous, rather that his righteousness creates works." First comes Christ's righteousness apprehended by faith alone, which Luther views as a gift from God, and then "the works follow." He emphasizes, "Works contribute nothing to justification." Yet, he also insists that "since Christ lives in us through faith so he arouses us to do good works."

This understanding raises the very important question for Luther of the relationship of law and grace. While we tend to emphasize the theology of the cross or the doctrines represented by the Reformation *solas,* Luther might well prefer we emphasize his understanding of law and grace as his enduring theological contribution. He once wrote, "Almost all Scripture and the understanding of all theology hangs on the proper understanding of law and gospel." Luther, not entirely in keeping with the other reformers, preferred to speak of only two uses of the law. The first use concerns the promotion of civic righteousness; we might prefer the term morality. This relates the law to the political sphere, or as Luther would term it, the "temporal estate." Here the law works positively to promote civility and preserve the order of God's creation.

The law's second use concerns the way it points us to Christ and boldly declares our need for his righteousness. He speaks of the law accusing us and condemning us, noting that its peculiar office "is to reprove sin and to lead to a knowledge of sin." In the *Smalcald Articles,* 1537, he refers to the law's chief function "to make original sin manifest, and show man to what utter depths his nature has fallen and how corrupt it has become." He further likens the law to a "thunderbolt by means of which God with one blow destroys both open sinners and false saints." It shows our inability to merit God's standard of righteousness, a realization that Luther had made early and often in his life, and our utter need for Christ's work.

The other reformers also considered a third use of the law, seeing it as a guide for Christians in the process of sanctification. Luther preferred to speak of the law as fulfilled in Christ and see the gospel as the guide for living the Christian life. The law works against us; the gospel works within us. As Luther notes, "The Law is the word of Moses to us, while the gospel is the word of God within us. The former remains outside and speaks of figures and visible shadows of things to come, but the latter comes inside and speaks of internal, spiritual, and true things." He also expresses similar thoughts in the *Heidelberg Disputation.* There he states, "The law says 'do this,' and it is never done. Grace says, 'believe in this,' and everything is done already." Again, it would be a mistake to think Luther endorsed a libertarian, or antinomian, approach to the Christian life. Luther simply avoids discussing the Christian's life of obedience as obedience to the law.

Luther's notion of *sola fide* and *sola gratia* naturally leads to the last of the Reformation *solas, solus Christus.* The doctrine of justification by faith alone highlights that the only mediator between God and a sinful humanity is the God-man, Christ (1 Tim. 2:5). Through an over-reliance on—and abuse of—the sacraments, through a misplaced trust in human ability, and through the emphasis on the indispensability of the Roman church, the fact that Christ alone reconciles humanity to God became obscured over the centuries of the medieval period. By Luther's day, Christ was largely crowded out altogether. Luther turned the focus off of these other concerns and returned it squarely to Christ. As he once remarked, "The center is Christ." This focus on Christ permeates Luther's writings. In his commentary on Romans 10:4, Luther writes, "Every word in the Bible points to Christ." Not surprisingly, he follows the implications of his own observation in his preaching. Consequently, a large majority of his sermons extol the person and work of Christ. We will see this theme in Luther's preaching more closely as we examine his sermon "On Christ's Holy Sufferings" in chapter 12.

Luther and the Laity

A discussion of Luther's theology would be incomplete without highlighting his theological breakthroughs regarding the laity's role. Luther's theological reforms also led to the reform of church practice and polity. This reform impacted a number of areas, such as preaching, music in the church, and church and state relations, all of which we will address in later chapters. The reforms also greatly impacted the laity. Two doctrines come to the fore here. First, Luther's idea of the priesthood of the believer overturned centuries of a hierarchical mindset that depreciated the laity, leaving it, and salvation, captive to the official church order. Contrary to the medieval Catholic view, Luther restored the view expressed in 1 Peter 2:5, which affirms that all believers constitute a "holy priesthood" and "[offer] spiritual sacrifices acceptable to God through Jesus Christ." As Luther exclaims, "Every shoemaker can be a priest of God." This priesthood grants access to God and his grace.

Again, however, careful understanding is in order. Luther did not abolish the clergy. In fact, he vehemently opposed the Anabaptists on this particular point. He maintained the necessity of a clergy, and a well-educated clergy at that, and of a church hierarchy. He rejected, however, any scheme that sets up one class, the priests, as having privileged and special access, relegating the rest of believers as second-class Christians. Medieval Catholic theology held to seven sacraments; among them stood ordination. Luther rejected ordination as a sacrament because he found no teaching of the priesthood as a sacrament in Scripture. He also rejected the implication intended by its being called a sacrament. As a sacrament, ordination extended a special grace not available to those outside the clergy. Luther instead observed, in his unique way, that you should only become a preacher if you "can believe that you are made not one whit better than the laity." These words come from his significant treatise in 1520, *The Babylonian Captivity of the Church*. There he also writes, "Let everyone, therefore, who knows himself to be a Christian, be assured of this, that we are all equally priests." For Luther, the office of the priesthood had to do solely with one's function in the church. As for one's relationship to or standing before God, he heralded the universal priesthood of all believers.

Secondly, Luther took the word "vocation," which means calling, and applied it to all occupations. This may not strike us as significant; yet, in the context of its day, it bears deep significance. The word vocation strictly applied to those taking monastic vows. This had a similar implication to that of designating the priesthood an ordinance, in that it granted a higher status to those taking the monastic vow than that available to those outside the monastery. This further implied that work outside of the monastery was less than a calling, with little if any spiritual significance. Consequently, Luther's view of applying the word vocation to all occupations signaled an entirely new perspective on work and daily, or so-called ordinary, life. All work, not just the churchly professions, could be done as an act of both service and worship. This concept actually may be summarized as another *sola, soli Deo gloria,* to the glory of God alone. This belief further enables all work, as well as all of life, to be viewed as bringing glory to God. Through these ideas of both the priesthood of the believer, as well as vocation, Luther chartered new and welcome waters for the church and the laity.

These theological contributions, deriving from various parts of his writings, were never viewed by Luther as his creation. He saw himself as simply declaring what was so plain in Scripture for all to see. "I did nothing," he once said, "the Word did it all." These doctrines, however obvious in the text, had nevertheless grown opaque, and the light of the Word had grown dim. Luther may not have created, but he did recover, both the source, Scripture, and the doctrines, especially the theology of the cross and the doctrine of justification by faith alone. In the chapters that follow we'll unpack these doctrines and examine the role they played in Luther's life and context, as well as the continuing impact they have for readers today. These doctrines, grounded in the Word of God, form the bedrock of our faith and play a defining role in our heritage. As we explore the context in which they developed, we should gain both a better understanding and a deeper appreciation of these fundamental truths. We continue our journey through the life and thought of Luther with these goals in mind.

A Note on the Sources

Works on Luther's theology will be discussed further in the conclusion. Four works in particular are quite helpful in understanding his theology. These include Bernard Lohse's *Martin Luther's Theology: Its Historical and Systematic*

Development (1999); Alister E. McGrath's *Luther's Theology of the Cross: Martin Luther's Theological Breakthrough* (1985); David C. Steinmetz's *Luther in Context* (1995); and Gerhard O. Forde's *On Being a Theologian of the Cross: Reflections on Luther's Heidelberg Disputation, 1518* (1997). Two other works offer a wide variety of Luther's writings on theology. These include Hugh Thomson Kerr's *A Compend of Luther's Theology* (1943) and Timothy F. Lull's *Martin Luther's Basic Theological Writings* (1989).

4

SILENT NO MORE

The Three Treatises

*"The whole world is blind and in great darkness;
only this man sees the truth."*
Johannes Bugenhagen, *upon reading*
The Babylonian Captivity of the Church

T HE TIME FOR SILENCE IS PAST, and the time to speak
has come." So writes Martin Luther in the preface
of his *To the Christian Nobility of the German Nation*,
the first of three writings commonly referred to as the *Three
Treatises*. Actually, Luther had been anything but silent for
the past few years. He first started speaking in 1517, and by
1520, continued to speak loudly. This year, 1520, marked a
watershed for the reformer. Earlier, he could have backed
down from his challenge to the pope, the indulgences, and
the entire Roman Catholic church. In fact, the events of the
fall months provided him with the very opportunity to do so.
Luther, however, stayed his course. Instead of backing down
during these months, he drove the wedge between himself

and the church deeper still. By the end of 1520, Luther's break with the church was all but final.

After the posting of the *Ninety-Five Theses*, Luther engaged in both pamphlet wars and debates with various church officials. His activity earned him a papal bull, or decree, in which he was condemned as a heretic. He responded, as only Luther could, by burning it publicly. He was not, however, simply another rebellious revolutionary. On the historical stage, his was a revolution of ideas, particularly the most significant of all ideas: those concerning humanity's relationship to God. So in addition to burning the papal decree, he took pen in hand and, during the fall months of 1520, wrote three works that stand prominently on any list of important Reformation writings. These include the already mentioned *Address to the Christian Nobility of the German Nation, The Babylonian Captivity of the Church,* and *The Freedom of the Christian.*

Tearing Down the Walls: *Address to the Christian Nobility*

Leo X, as mentioned earlier, issued his decree against Luther on June 15, 1520. It offered Luther two choices: he could recant, or he could refuse to recant and be declared a heretic. Luther had sixty days from the time he received the decree to decide. He received it on October 10, and on December 10 he burned it. Before even receiving the bull, he wrote the first of his *Three Treatises* in late August 1520. Next followed *Babylonian Captivity* in October, and then the third installment, *The Freedom of the Christian,* came off the press in November.

In the first of the *Three Treatises,* Luther sets about the essential, but quite unpopular, task of tearing down the walls built by Rome that held the German nation and its inhabitants captive. He uses this imagery of the walls to impress upon his primary audience, the princes and rulers of Germany or the "Nobility of the German nation," the extraordinary power that Rome unrightfully exercises over their lands. The first wall, which Luther refers to as a "pure invention," concerns the radical distinction within the medieval church between church officials and laity. According to this view the pope, bishops, priests, and monks belong to the higher "spiritual state," while state officials, artisans, merchants, farmers, and peasants—everybody else, in other words—crawl about in the lower "temporal state." In other words, the clergy-laity distinction ran so deeply that all on the laity side were viewed as inferior, and certainly less spiritual than those on the other side.

This disparity reveals much about the medieval world and the greater world on the eve of the Reformation. The church had risen in power ever since the beginning of the medieval period. In 800, Pope Leo III crowned Charlemagne Emperor of the Holy Roman Empire. This fact is significant for several reasons, but essentially it reveals the power of the papacy, as it signifies, by the pope's crowning, that the state was to bow before the church. To be sure, this power waxed and waned throughout the medieval period, due largely to the abilities of the pope at any given time. One thing stands clear, however, and that is the political power of the church. In addition to this political power, one also sees the spiritual power the church exercised. The sacraments, covering the cradle to the grave—from baptism to last rites—belonged exclusively to the church and its officials. And, consequently, so did salvation. Those outside the so-called priestcraft, or those other than the bishops, clergy, and monks, were entirely dependent upon the church and its officials for salvation.

Luther proposed to tear down this wall by emphasizing

the various biblical teachings concerning the body of Christ and the priesthood of believers. We are all members of one body, Luther stated, echoing Paul's sentiment, and "every member has his own work by which he serves others." This equipping of the saints is not because of our office, but rather because "we all have one baptism, one gospel, one faith, and are all Christians alike." Luther adds that the popes and bishops may anoint, shave the heads of the monks, ordain and consecrate, but they "can never make a man into a Christian or into a spiritual man by so doing." He continues colorfully, "He might well make a man into a hypocrite, a humbug, or a blockhead, but never a Christian or a spiritual man." Instead, Luther points to Peter's words observing that we are all, as Christians, consecrated priests (1 Peter 2:9).

Luther clearly acknowledges that different believers serve different functions within the body of Christ. He also emphasizes the clergy's need to guide believers in both biblical understanding and in living the Christian life. In fact, once Luther's movement got underway, he sharply criticized those, such as his colleague at Wittenberg, Andreas Karlstadt, for their attempts to abolish any distinctions altogether. He argued "that there is no true, basic difference between laymen and priests, princes and bishops, between religious and secular, except for the sake of office and work, but not for the sake of status." Luther still sees a viable role for the clergy that is different from that of the laity. But as far as one's status goes, or, for that matter, as far as one's ability to live a life that is pleasing to God, Luther proposes to tear down any such wall of distinction.

The second wall concerns Scripture and the control that the "Romanists" exercised over it. Here he directly attacks the claim that only the pope can rightly interpret Scripture for the church, as well as the claim that the church is the guardian of the true interpretation. As Luther observes, "The

Romanists want to be the masters of Holy Scripture, although they never learn a thing from the Bible. They assume the sole authority for themselves, and, quite unashamed, they play about with the words before our very eyes, trying to persuade us that the pope cannot err in matters of faith." Luther explains how these ideas have gone unchallenged, noting that many, including himself, have never looked at the Bible long enough to see the baselessness of Rome's view. When Luther did read the Bible, he realized the deception and exclaimed, "I would not have believed it possible for the devil to have made such stupid claims as Rome, and to have won supporters for them." Luther concludes that an office is not authoritative; only the text is.

The third wall builds on the previous one and declares that papal authority is unquestionable, a concept also known as papal infallibility. Luther appeals to the domino effect: if the first two walls collapse, then so should this one. As he observes, "The third wall falls of itself when the first two are down." Scripture is infallible, but the pope is not. In fact, he notes, when "the pope is an offense to Christendom," then the first one who is able should speak out against him. He adds that "when the pope acts contrary to the Scriptures, it is our duty to stand by the Scriptures, to reprove him and constrain him."

Luther's Fool's Song

Luther emphasizes these three walls to send a wake-up call to the leaders of Germany. In the reformer's view, these leaders had both an ethical and a spiritual obligation to the people of their lands. And, in Luther's opinion, the current state of affairs had reached crisis proportions. This was not only true on the spiritual count, but also on the social and political one, as Luther reminds the princes:

Some have estimated that more than three hundred thousand gulden a year find their way from Germany to Rome. This money serves no use or purpose. We get nothing for it except scorn and contempt. And we still go on wondering why princes and nobles, cities and endowments, land and people grow poor. We ought to marvel that we have anything left to eat!

Luther concludes that papal Rome is the very center "of avarice and robbery." He likens it to "a brothel above all imaginable brothels," where "all dishonesty and shame can be made to look like honor and glory." The princes, Luther contends, facilitate all of this activity by not taking a stand against Rome. These economic abuses are only the beginning, however, for the true travesty concerns the spiritual darkness that not only overhangs Rome, but engulfs Germany as well. Having thoroughly laid out the contemporary situation for Germany, Luther proposes what should be done. He prefaces his prescription with the following remarks: "Now, although I am too insignificant a man to make propositions for the improvement of this dreadful state of affairs, nevertheless I shall sing my fool's song through to the end and say, as far as I am able, what could and should be done." When Luther said that he would sing his "fool's song to the end," he was not jesting, as he lays out no fewer than twenty-seven separate points of advice for the German nobility. He addresses everything from church practice to the administration of universities. He also challenges the princes themselves for some of their business interests and commercial practices.

Although it was close to biting the hand that feeds him, Luther, nevertheless, did not back down where his convictions caused him to make a stand. One area, in particular, that concerned Luther involved the rise of banks and lending practices. He wrote, "What I really cannot understand is how a man with one hundred gulden can make a profit of twenty in one year. Nor, for that matter, can I understand how a man with one gulden can make another—and all this not from toiling the soil or raising cattle." He then reveals his economic theory, observing, "I know full well that it would be a far more godly thing to increase agriculture and decrease commerce." While not all agreed with his theory, what Luther attempted to do here was to force the nobility to think through the implications of their practices for the poor and the common good. Ultimately, Luther wanted the German nobles to realize that being a Christian meant being a Christian noble and carrying out this temporal office governed by Christian principles. He then closed with his hope for the German nation as expressed in a short prayer: "God give us a Christian mind, and grant to the Christian nobility of the German nation in particular true spiritual courage to do the best they can for the poor church."

The Babylonian Captivity of the Church

Luther's fool's song did not end with the completion of his address to the German nobility. He carried on that song for many decades. But in the following few months, he continued focusing on the urgent issues facing him. Sacramentalism captured Luther's attention in the second installment of the *Three Treatises*. Luther's quarrel with Rome started over his concerns for the abuse of one sacrament in particular, penance. The church's practice of this sacrament brought forth Luther's stinging critique in the *Ninety-Five Theses*. He continued lobbing salvos at the abuse of that sacrament, as well as at the other sacraments, in various sermons throughout the years 1517–1519. By the time he wrote *The Babylonian Captivity of the Church* in 1520, he launched a full-scale attack. Anybody even vaguely familiar with Scripture will know that the designation "Babylon" is not a compliment. When Luther couples it with the word "captivity," his intention is even less ambiguous. His challenge to the church included two main features. First, he reduced the number of sacraments from seven to two. Next, he radically reshaped the remaining two.

Before he starts his critique, he shows us how his thinking has changed on this from his earlier days. Obviously, as a monk, he followed the church's practice, but soon he realized that such practice was not true to Scripture. He references the *Ninety-Five Theses* and his work that immediately followed, *Explanations of the Ninety-Five Theses,* but quickly added an apology for the work, not because it was critical, but because it did not go far enough. He wrote, "I now deeply regret having published that little book." Mainly because, at the time, he "still clung with a mighty superstition to the tyranny of Rome," he did not reject indulgences altogether, calling for their reform instead. But his mind changed, and he wanted the record to be clear. He stated, in capital letters no less, "INDULGENCES ARE WICKED DEVICES OF THE FLATTERERS OF ROME."

While he rejected indulgences, he nevertheless argued for the validity of penance or confession. Now Luther's treatise is not the clearest on this point. To be sure, he thoroughly discusses how far the current practice of penance drifted from the biblical teaching of confession. Nevertheless, during his treatment of penance, he seems to refer to it as a valid sacrament. At the end of the treatise he wrote, "Hence there are, strictly speaking, but two sacraments in the church of God—baptism and the bread." He then refers to penance as "nothing but a way and return to baptism." Yet, when he writes the *Small Catechism* in 1529, he includes a section on confession in between sections on baptism and the Lord's

Supper. Perhaps we can clear up the ambiguity by concluding that Luther holds to two sacraments only, baptism and communion, while also seeing a crucial and necessary place for confession. Luther's emphasis on confession might come as a surprise to contemporary Protestants. Before we cast judgment on Luther for his understanding of confession, however, a look at what he intended proves helpful. We will return to this in chapter eight when we examine his mature thought on this subject in *The Small Catechism*.

Understanding the Sacraments

As mentioned earlier, the two sacraments that Luther retained come to appear quite different than they do in the Roman scheme. Before he begins reshaping them along the lines of biblical teaching, he first discusses his overall perspective on the sacraments by way of introduction. He turns next to the sacraments beginning first with, as he refers to it in the customary language of the medieval period, the sacrament of the bread, moving next to baptism, and then to penance. He spends the bulk of his time addressing the abuses of these sacraments and explaining how such abuse harms the laity. He argues that the church, abusing its power, has taken these sacraments captive, causing the laity to miss out on their blessing. He follows this by examining the four sacraments of Roman Catholicism that he rejects as unwarranted by Scripture, treating confirmation, ordination, marriage, and last rites (extreme unction) successively.

The fundamental role and nature of the sacraments permeates this writing. The Roman church held that the sacraments are, in fact, much more than mere signs, as they are in themselves means of grace. The Roman church over time further developed the notion that the sacraments function in an automatic fashion. The Latin expression for this is *ex opere operato,* literally meaning that the sacraments work (operate) by the mere act of their working. This troubled Luther as he viewed the sacraments as signs pointing to both Christ, whom Luther refers to at the beginning of the treatise as the one and only true sacrament, and faith in Christ. Now Luther does not arrive at the same conclusion as Ulrich Zwingli, who viewed the sacraments, and especially the Lord's Supper, as a memorial only. In fact, Luther and his followers break with Zwingli and his followers over this very issue. What Luther emphasizes, and what he found missing in the Roman view, is "the word of divine promise in the sacrament."

He explains what he meant by this as he wrote, "God does not deal, nor has he ever dealt with man otherwise than through a word of promise. We in turn cannot deal with God other than through faith in the Word of his promise." He then observes that the biblical pattern reveals how God adds a sign to the promise. For instance, the promise that God makes to Abraham in Genesis 12–15 is followed by the sign of circumcision in Genesis 17. And so it is with the Lord's Supper, as it, too, is a sign of the promise. Now the sign is important, but not in and of itself. Instead, what matters is what the sign points to, and even more than that, faith in what the sign points to. As Luther concludes, "Hence the only worthy preparation and proper observance is faith, the faith by which we believe in the Lord's Supper, that is, in the divine promise." Instead of condoning Rome's view that the sacraments work automatically, Luther heralds that the sacraments are effective only as exercised by faith. Once again, Luther makes this clear:

> For this treatment of Christ [in the sacrament] is the one remedy against sins, past, present, and future, if you but cling to it with unwavering faith and believe that what the

words of the sacrament declare is freely granted to you. But if you do not believe this, you will never anywhere, by any works or efforts on your own, be able to find peace of conscience. For faith alone means peace of conscience, while unbelief only means distress of conscience.

Luther's view on the sacraments reveals the centrality of faith in his theology. It further shows how far Rome had drifted from the biblical teaching, obscuring the sacraments' true role. Beyond this fundamental criticism of the abuse of the sacraments, Luther also offers numerous specific criticisms of the practice of all seven. For example, the Roman view of the Lord's Supper was that the congregation only partook of the bread, while the priest alone partook of the cup, explaining why it was referred to as the sacrament of bread in the Middle Ages. Luther finds here a clear case of the church substituting its authority and practice in place of Scripture. In fact, this charge pervades the treatise and forms the substance of his arguments against the validity of the other four so-called sacraments. Luther's view, simply stated, holds that only that which is divinely instituted counts as a sacrament. Luther underscores a profit motive behind the sacramental system of the medieval church. At one point he observes that the sacraments have been "turned into mere merchandise, a market, and a profit-making business."

Luther wrote this treatise in Latin, evidence that he aimed it not at a popular audience, but at a scholarly one, and that he intended it to spark discussion among scholars. It did just that. Aleander, the papal secretary who became Luther's nemesis, quickly attempted to refute it as blasphemy. Other Roman church officials ironically both suppressed it and distributed it widely, the one action attempting to keep his heresy from spreading, the other attempting to reveal how heretical Luther in fact was. Upon reading it, Erasmus noted, "The

Fig. 4.1 Luther's Decisive Year (1520)

June 15	Pope Leo X issues Papal Bull *"Exsurge, Domine"*
Aug.	Writes *Address to the Christian Nobility of the German Nation*
Oct.	Writes *The Babylonian Captivity of the Church*
Nov.	Writes *The Freedom of the Christian*
Nov.	Writes *Against the Detestable Bull of the Antichrist*
Dec. 10	Publicly burns the Papal Bull

breach is irreparable," acknowledging the extent of the differences between Luther and Rome. Henry VIII, before he himself broke from Rome and established the Anglican Church, ordered the book to be burned and wrote a lengthy criticism against it. Pope Leo X gave Henry VIII the title "Defender of the Faith" for his attack on Luther—an action which later popes, dealing with Henry VIII during the 1530s, more than likely deeply regretted. Not all of the response was negative, as some, such as Johannes Bugenhagen, found Luther's words convincing and joined with him because of the work. Luther's criticism of the church in the year 1520, however, had not yet come to an end, as he would have one final installment.

The Power of Faith: *The Freedom of the Christian*

Luther begins the last and shortest of the *Three Treatises, The Freedom of a Christian,* November 1520, with a paradox, as he writes,

> A Christian is a perfectly free lord of all, subject to none.
> A Christian is a perfectly dutiful servant of all, subject to all.

He immediately admits the seeming contradiction in these claims. He points out, however, that he did not invent this paradox, but rather that it derives from the teachings of

Paul in 1 Corinthians 9:19. Luther further finds within this paradox the key to understanding the whole Christian life. This is because, for Luther, being both free and a servant expresses the proper relationship of faith and works.

He, of course, starts off with faith, or Christian freedom, pointing out that "one thing, and only one thing, is necessary for Christian life, righteousness, and freedom. That one thing is the most holy Word of God, the gospel of Christ." With no veiled reference to his contemporary situation, he observes that "there is no more terrible disaster with which the wrath of God can afflict man than a famine of the hearing of his Word." But, "there is no greater mercy than when God sends forth his Word." Luther explains what he means by the Word of God, which he, referencing Romans 1, summarizes as "the gospel of God concerning his Son, who was made flesh, suffered, rose from the dead, and was glorified through the Spirit who sanctifies. To preach Christ means to feed the soul, make it righteous, set it free, and save it." He quickly adds that the Word of God cannot be received any way other than by faith. "This faith," he continues, "cannot exist in connection with works." Consequently, "wherefore it ought to be the first concern of every Christian to lay aside all confidence in works and increasingly strengthen faith alone and through faith to grow in the knowledge, not of works, but of Jesus Christ" (1 Peter 5:10).

Faith, according to Luther, reveals our own desperate need. It shows us how unworthy we are of God's righteousness, how sinful we are, and how incapable we are of remedying our situation. We learn this as we see "that the entire Scripture of God is divided into two parts: commandments and promises." We learn through the commandments "to recognize [our] helplessness . . . to be humbled and reduced to nothing." But then the promises of God, that "are holy, true, righteous, free, and peaceful words, full of goodness," come to our aid. In other words, we learn from the promises to rely solely upon the work of God. Luther presents this as the "first power of faith." The "second power of faith" is that faith fosters trust, and trust fosters obedience. Luther expresses it this way: "The very highest worship is this, that we ascribe to him truthfulness, righteousness, and whatever else should be ascribed to one who is trusted. When this is done, the soul consents to his will." This trust in God not only fosters obedience, but also fosters rest and contentment in God's plan. Again Luther observes that the one who clings to God in faith "does not doubt that he who is true, just, and wise will do, dispose, and provide all things well."

The third power of faith concerns the union of the "soul with Christ as a bride is united with her bridegroom." This union frees us from the power of sin, secures us from death and hell, and endows us with eternal life. This is true

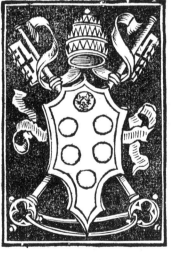

Courtesy of the Pitts Theology Library, Candler School of Theology

4.2 Title page of Leo X's 1520 Papal Bull against the errors of Martin Luther.

freedom, and it comes only by faith. That being the case, Luther raises the question of the role of works. While he argues that we don't perform works to become righteous, he also contends that we "must do works freely only to please God." Returning to the second power of faith, obedience to God's commands naturally derives from trust in God. Works similarly are a natural response of gratitude to the work that God has done. Luther is clear: "We do not, therefore, reject good works; on the contrary, we cherish and teach them as much as possible." For Luther, however, both the order and nature of works must be firmly established. They follow faith, and they are a grateful response of those made righteous by faith, not a prerequisite for righteousness.

Free to Serve

One further role of works concerns Christians' service toward their neighbors. As Luther states, "A man does not live for himself alone in this mortal body to work for it alone, but he lives also for all men on earth; rather, he lives only for others and not for himself." Luther then returns to the paradox with which he opened this treatise. We are perfectly free in Christ. In fact, Luther even says that we are more free than kings. Yet, we are bound to serve our neighbor. In other words: we serve all because we are free. Luther sees this servanthood in the example of Christ as given by Paul in Philippians 2. Christ, the God-man possessing the riches of heaven, became a servant. Luther makes the application to the Christian:

> Although the Christian is thus free from all works, he ought in this liberty to empty himself, take upon himself the form of a servant, be made in the likeness of men, be found in human form, and to serve, help, and in every

way deal with his neighbor as he sees God through Christ has dealt with him and still deals with him.

Ironically, Luther dedicated the Latin version of this work to Pope Leo X. Perhaps he meant it as a conciliatory token. In his dedicatory letter, he writes that *The Freedom of a Christian* is a small book, but "unless I am mistaken, however, it contains the whole of Christian life in brief form, provided you grasp its meaning." This little book, with its short paradox and its extensive discussion of faith, speaks volumes on living the Christian life. Luther helps us, as he does in so many of his writings, to understand the centrality and nature of faith. He further helps us see the proper role that works play in our life. This work and the two other works comprising the *Three Treatises* sparked a firestorm in Luther's day. Though much of the material relates directly to Luther's situation, especially the first two treatises, these works still have much to offer contemporary Christians seeking to understand how to bring the Bible to bear upon the challenges of the day and to understand what it means to live the Christian life.

A Note on the Sources

The *Three Treatises* may be found in the following volumes in *Luther's Works*: *Volume 44, The Christian in Society I,* "To The Christian Nobility of the German Nation" (1966), edited by James Atkinson, pages 115–217; *Volume 36, Word and Sacrament II,* "The Babylonian Captivity of the Church" (1959), edited by Abdel Ross Wentz, pages 3–126; and *Volume 31, Career of the Reformer I,* "The Freedom of a Christian" (1957), edited by Harold J. Grimm, pages 327–77. Each text is accompanied by a helpful introduction. These works have also been published together in a single volume in Martin Luther's *Three Treatises* (1970).

5

THE CENTERPIECE
OF THE REFORMATION

The Bondage of the Will

"There is nothing easier than sinning."
Martin Luther

L UTHER ONCE REMARKED that his persecutors could burn all of his books except two. While the pope took him literally, he nevertheless failed to grant Luther his wish. Thankfully, we do not have to content ourselves with only two of Luther's books. If we had to do so, however, Luther informs us which two we *should* have: *The Small Catechism* and *The Bondage of the Will*. The range of these two works illustrates Luther's remarkable abilities. *The Small Catechism,* with its clarity and economy of words, presents a concise statement of the essentials of Christian practice and doctrine for young and old alike. Understandable, challenging, and provocative simultaneously, it clearly ranks among the classics of Christian literature.

And then there is *The Bondage of the Will*. Unlike the shorter work, *The Small Catechism,* this work is a treatise, presenting a theological tour de force. Here we see Luther's mind at its sharpest, tackling the perennial theological challenge of engaging the relationship between human freedom and responsibility on the one hand, and God's sovereignty on the other. Luther's insightful treatment of the issue also serves to rank this text among the classics of the Christian tradition, as well. He knew of the importance of both *The Small Catechism* and *The Bondage of the Will,* not because he wrote them, but because of the issues they addressed. He more than likely, however, had no idea that his thoughts would continue to be helpful to Christians wrestling with these ideas centuries later.

Luther's choice of *The Bondage of the Will* further makes sense when we understand his perspective on the issues it addresses. He considered these issues of human freedom and ability to be at the very heart of the Reformation. This became clear to him as he engaged the work of Desiderius Erasmus, the great Greek scholar and Luther's contemporary. Luther's book, *The Bondage of the Will,* actually presents a response to Erasmus's work bearing the opposing title, *On the Freedom of the Will*. Erasmus wrote this work in response to shorter writings and sermons of Luther. Consequently, when we read *The Bondage of the Will,* we are listening in on a debate between two of the most prominent intellectuals of the sixteenth century. To understand Luther's arguments in the book, we first need to look to Erasmus and his interaction with Luther. In the following pages, we will engage the debate between Erasmus and Luther. We will also explore Luther's ideas in this classic text, what J. I. Packer has called "the greatest piece to come from Luther's pen." Luther's text, however, is not simply a polemical treatise. In other words, it moves beyond merely criticizing Erasmus, as it offers some rather positive and profitable insight.

Luther and Erasmus

Desiderius Erasmus of Rotterdam, 1466–1536, represents the quintessential Renaissance scholar. Highly educated, Erasmus was ordained as a priest, but he never performed the duties of one. Instead, he devoted his life to academia, holding a prestigious post at the University of Cambridge

Courtesy of the Pitts Theology Library, Candler School of Theology

ERASMVS ROTERODAMVS BATAVVS

Ingens ingentem quem perſonat orbis Eraſmum
Hac tibi dimidium, picta tabella refert.
At curnon totum? mirari deſine, lec̄tor,
Integro nam tantum terra nec ipſa capit.

C

5.1 Portrait of Desiderius Erasmus, whose work promoting the view of free will prompted Luther's *The Bondage of the Will*.

and ranking as the day's most learned and witty writer. He also traveled frequently throughout Europe, enjoying the benefits his reputation brought him. He offered a sharp and sustained criticism of the church on two fronts. First, his classic work written in 1509, *The Praise of Folly,* offers a sarcastic and deeply penetrating portrayal of much of life in the sixteenth century, including scholars who take themselves too seriously. He saves his sharpest censure for the clergy and its widespread corruption and even ignorance. In other words, in concert with Luther, he viewed the church to be in dire need of reform.

Erasmus's other well-known work also resonates with Luther. Erasmus spent nearly ten years in his travels and at Cambridge collecting and collating the various Greek manuscripts housed in monasteries throughout Europe. Prior to his efforts, a Greek text of the New Testament, drawing from the rich manuscript tradition, simply did not exist. He published his text in 1516 at Basel. Here we see Erasmus ranking among the best of the humanist scholars, as he moves beyond the Latin translation of the Bible, and, in the spirit of the Renaissance motto, *ad fontes,* "to the fount," going straight to the source, the Greek New Testament. This event, coupled with Luther's simultaneous dissatisfaction with the church, serves as the catalyst for the Reformation and its spread. Luther employed Erasmus's text for his German translation of the Bible, and it serves as the Greek text behind the tradition of the English Bible. A copy of the text fell into the hands of Ulrich Zwingli the same year it was published. After studying it diligently, Zwingli decided to begin preaching through the Bible in Zurich in 1520. He started with Matthew 1:1, and over time, he catapulted the city of Zurich into the Reformation.

Erasmus's text made an extraordinary impact on the Reformation. Today, textual criticism scholars have pointed to some flaws in his methodology, and since 1516, other ancient manuscripts have been discovered that have changed the face of the discipline of textual criticism. Erasmus, however, pioneered the return to the original text. These two issues, the focus on the biblical text and the criticism of the church, met with hearty approval by Luther and even inspired his work further. The two men met as Erasmus made extended visits to Wittenberg. Yet, as he engaged Erasmus, Luther soon realized that while they agreed that reform was necessary, they disagreed over what shape the reform should take and how far it should extend.

Luther expressed both his admiration and his concern for Erasmus in a letter to Johann Lang. In one sentence he sums up both Erasmus's strength and shortcoming: "I am pleased that he exposes and attacks the ignorance of the monks and the priests, but I fear that he does not sufficiently promote Christ and the grace of God." On another occasion, he observes that Erasmus "knows nothing" of the gospel. At one point Luther declares, "Erasmus never has anything to say about justification," adding, "he irritated and put down the papacy and now he draws his head out of the noose." As Luther pulled back his support for Erasmus, so Erasmus distanced himself from the reformer. Erasmus remained in the Catholic church, though his commitment never moved much beyond a nominal expression.

The two men had their most extended discussion over the issue of the will. The theological discussion over the will, however, began long before they entered the fray and continues long past their work. In fact, shortly after Luther's debate with Erasmus, the issues were recast along the lines of the Arminian and Calvinist controversy. The roots of the debate also extend back to the early church to Augustine and the Pelagian controversy. As Erasmus notes in the opening lines of *On the Freedom of the Will: A Discourse,* "Among the difficulties, of which not a few crop up in Holy Scripture, there is hardly a more tangled labyrinth than that of 'free choice,' for it is a subject that has long exercised the minds of philosophers, and also of theologians of old and new, in a striking degree, though in my opinion with more labor than fruit." Erasmus then notes in the preface of the *Discourse* that Luther has "violently stirred up" the issue, and, even though reluctant, he felt compelled to respond.

Erasmus's Challenge

Erasmus echoes Pelagius's contention concerning the doctrine of original sin. Pelagius, a late fourth- and early fifth-century monk, grew increasingly troubled over the lax morality rampant in the church of his day. He viewed the problem as stemming directly from Augustine's teaching on original sin. In short, this doctrine, following Paul's teaching in Romans 5:12–21, teaches that Adam's fall plunged humanity into sin. Consequently, sin is not in the sinning, but in being a sinner. In other words, because of Adam's fall, one is a sinner long before one sins. Augustine draws the implication then that no one seeks God's favor and that no one is in any way capable of meriting God's favor. Consequently, God chooses us, as Christ informs the crowd gathered to hear his teaching in John 6:44, "No one can come to me unless the Father who sent me draws him," or as Christ later tells the disciples in John 15:16, "You did not choose me, but I chose you."

Pelagius saw such teaching, and its emphasis on human inability, as not tending to promote morality. Additionally, the teaching that God holds humans responsible for the sin of Adam strikes even the most casual observer as utterly unfair and unjust. Pelagius then reaches a different conclusion than Augustine did. He sees Adam as simply our example and nothing more. Consequently, one's ability to merit God's favor and capacity to choose God's favor are intact. According to Pelagius, in order for God to be fair, we must be free. The church rejected Pelagianism, but never fully. By the time of the early 1500s, Erasmus revived basic Pelagian tenets; Luther sided with Augustine. Before Erasmus wrote his challenge to Luther, the reformer expressed his ideas in various writings. Erasmus sees great danger in Luther's defense of the Augustinian view. In fact, he notes that promoting these views "opens a window to impiety." Erasmus then challenged Luther by teaching that Scripture and the church fathers put forth the following definition: "By free choice in this place we mean a power of the human will by which a man can apply himself to the things which lead to eternal salvation, or turn away from them."

Erasmus held that the fall negatively impacted the will. Nevertheless, the light is not so dim that one cannot use it properly. He also emphatically stresses the need for God's grace. But he prefers to speak of God's grace and human ability in cooperation to achieve salvation. To assert such cooperation strikes Erasmus as perfectly in keeping with Scripture and doing full justice to God's glory in the act of redemption. He writes, "I ask what merit can a man arrogate to himself if whatever, as a man, he is able to achieve by his natural intelligence and free choice, all this he owes to the one from whom he receives these powers." Erasmus understood his view as not offensive to God's sovereignty and majesty. Luther could not disagree more.

Luther's Response

We may well recall that Luther kept busy during the summer and fall months of 1525. He was married in June and contended with the Peasants' War, writing extensively on the subject. These matters delayed the typical speedy response to Erasmus's challenge. Because of the delay, popular opinion expressed that Luther had finally met his match. Luther, however, explains his delay in the introduction and proceeds to respond. Before he even leaves the introduction, he offers the reader a summary of his response: "The plain evidence is that free choice is a pure fiction." Luther's treatise provides a detailed response to Erasmus's argument. He spends some time engaging Erasmus's preface and introduction, addressing methodological and foundational issues before he turns to the issue at hand. The middle section of the book continues to focus on Erasmus's arguments. By the end, Luther moves from being specifically tied to such arguments to addressing Paul and John's teaching on the issue.

One of the points of Erasmus's argument concerns our ability to understand Scripture. He contends that much of Scripture is obscure and difficult to understand. Consequently, we should content ourselves with its basic teachings and avoid getting into it too deeply. He applies this to the argument at hand by relegating the question of the will to the periphery. This elicits quite a response from Luther. In the process of replying, Luther sets forth a very different understanding of both Scripture and doctrine.

Erasmus viewed Scripture more opaquely than did Luther. Erasmus likened Scripture to the mythological cave of Corycos. The deeper one descends into the cave, the "darker and darker it becomes." So it is with Scripture. The more one plumbs its depths, the less one appreciates God and the further away God moves. Erasmus further applied this approach as his method of theology. He wanted a rather defined center of belief, leaving the rest shrouded in "mystic silence." Erasmus included the question of the will in this latter category, which explains his reluctance to write on it. Luther agrees that there are mysteries to the Christian faith. He draws the line in a quite different location, however. Consequently, when it comes to crucial doctrines that reflect large portions of biblical teaching, Luther would not, like Erasmus, "discourse." Instead, Luther asserted. This assertion is not based on human bravado, but rather on the certainty of God's Word. "I am speaking," Luther explains, "about the assertion of those things which have been divinely transmitted to us in the sacred writings." These doctrines are for Luther the essence of Christianity. As he states, "Take away assertions and you take away Christianity."

Luther further explains that "the subject matter of the Scriptures, therefore, is all quite accessible, even though some texts are still obscure owing to our ignorance of their terms." He expresses the accessibility of Scripture as the doctrine of both the internal and external clarity of Scripture. By external clarity, Luther essentially means that Scripture, conveyed in ordinary human language and employing human customs, may be read and understood. As for the internal clarity, this engages the Holy Spirit's ministry of enabling us to understand Scripture. Luther observes, "If you speak of the internal clarity, no man perceives one iota of what is in the Scriptures unless he has the Spirit of God. . . . For the Spirit is required for the understanding of all Scripture and every part of Scripture." Consequently, Luther rejects Erasmus's skeptical approach to establishing the boundaries and parameters of Scripture's teaching on the issue of the will.

As Luther observes, Erasmus considers the "subject of free choice among the things that are useless and unnecessary," instead supplying a list of things that he "considers sufficient for the Christian religion." Luther notices that Erasmus fails to mention Christ on the list, exclaiming to Erasmus directly, "as if you think that Christian godliness can exist without Christ so long as God is worshipped with all one's powers as being by nature most merciful." The assertion concerning free will stands, according to Luther, at the heart of the matter. And, as he continues his response, we will see why this is the case. At this point in *The Bondage of the Will,* it is not Erasmus's actual view of free choice that bothers Luther. Rather, it is the way that Erasmus relegates the issue to the periphery that troubles him. Such an indifferent approach to crucial theological issues again reveals the deeply rooted differences between the humanist scholar and the reformer. Once Erasmus unfolds his understanding of the will, however, that, too, deeply troubles Luther, and he responds at length in the rest of the pages of *The Bondage of the Will.*

The Sinful Lump

Luther begins his final major section of the treatise with Paul's teaching in Romans 1. Here Luther understands Paul as presenting humanity standing under God's wrath and in dire need of the gospel. Luther concludes from this that "Paul in this passage lumps all men in a single mass, and concludes that, so far from being able to will or do anything good, they are all ungodly, wicked, and ignorant of righteousness and faith." Purposefully using the language of "single mass," Luther reflects the similar interpretation of this passage by Augustine. Augustine understood the argument of Romans as presenting humanity as a "sinful mass," or "sinful lump." In other words, all of humanity stands condemned before God, united to their head, Adam. Out of this sinful mass, Augustine argues, God chose another mass of people who would be united to the second Adam, Christ. This understanding reflects the doctrines of the imputation of sin, as Adam's act of disobedience gets credited to all of humanity's account, and the imputation of Christ's righteousness, as Christ's act of obedience gets credited to the account of those who believe in him.

Returning to Luther: This mass of humanity stands under God's wrath and is ignorant of him. Luther then reveals the implication for human ability: "For this means that in themselves they are ignorant, and being ignorant of the righteousness of salvation, they are certainly under wrath and damnation, from which in their ignorance, they can neither extricate themselves nor even try to." Humanity is not free and able, but bound and unable. This conviction also helps us understand Luther when he speaks against freedom. He does not posit determinism. In fact, Luther is quick to relate free will to what he terms "life below." In one of his "Table Talk" selections he notes that free will "milks cows and builds houses." In *The Bondage of the Will,* Luther defines "free will" as the ability to orient ourselves toward God or to merit his work in our lives. In other words, free will has to do with ability, or better inability. And the best way to understand this inability comes in the words of Paul in Romans 3:10–11 as he cites Psalm 14: "There is no one righteous, not even one; there is no one who understands, no one who seeks God."

Luther asks Erasmus the penetrating question, "How can they strive after the good, when they are totally ignorant of God and neither seek after God nor pay any regard to him?" Further, Luther contends that on our own, we would not even be aware that we are sinners. He understands John 16:8 to teach that humanity remains ignorant not only of Christ, but also of sin "until the convincing Spirit reveals it." He concludes that the will is free, that is free to sin. Unlike Erasmus, Luther does not celebrate this human trait. Rather, he sees that it reveals our desperation and need.

While much of Luther's argument is clear, even at times colorfully stated in his inimitable way, his conclusion sufficiently sums up the argument in a straightforward manner. He offers five reasons Erasmus's position falters. First, he points to the sovereignty of God, as he writes, "If we believe it to be true that God foreknows and predestines all things, that he can neither be mistaken in his foreknowledge, nor hindered in his predestination, and nothing takes place but as he wills it, then on the testimony of reason itself there cannot be any free choice in man." His second reason concerns Satan, the god of this world. Because he is "forever plotting and fighting against the kingdom of Christ . . . there can be no such thing as free choice." Thirdly, he notes that "If we believe that original sin has so ruined us that even in those who are led by the Spirit it causes a great deal of trouble by struggling against the good, it is clear that in a man devoid of the Spirit there is nothing left that can turn toward the good, but only toward evil." His fourth reason concerns the surprising work of God. He notices how Jews, who vigorously pursued righteousness, "ran headlong into unrighteousness." Gentiles, conversely, "pursued ungodliness [and] attained righteousness freely and unexpectedly."

His fifth reason concerns the cross. He observes, "If we believe that Christ has redeemed men by his blood, we are bound to confess that the whole man was lost." It may be recalled that Erasmus, following Pelagius, held that the fall did not extinguish humanity's reasoning capacities. This last point challenges that notion. It also connects Luther's argument in *The Bondage of the Will* to his central motif of the theology of the cross. Ultimately, Luther vehemently opposed Erasmus because he promoted a "theology of glory," disparaging the theology of the cross. In other words, Erasmus's view promotes an unhealthy exaltation of the self and its role in salvation, stemming from a misplaced trust in human ability. Luther reminds us that the cross is God's "No" to human ability. Again, we see the importance of this issue for Luther as the understanding of human nature and the will relates entirely to grasping what Christ was doing on the cross.

The Centerpiece of the Reformation

Luther argues that salvation was exclusively a work of God and that nothing that we can do will avail for our salvation. He also asserts the necessity of belief, understood by Luther as a gift of God. Consequently, he stresses human inability and God's infinite ability as he articulates a view of salvation that reserves the praise, honor, and glory entirely and exclusively for God alone. Perhaps the one element of Erasmus with which we would agree concerns his observation that the discussion surrounding this debate tends to promote more labor than fruit. As Luther's work not only impacts the discussion in his day, but continues to do so even in ours, we see one of those rare occasions of fruit, of light, and not just heat.

The Bondage of the Will, and the debate with Erasmus, reveals much about Luther's perspective on the nature of the Reformation. He, like Erasmus, expressed deep concern regarding problems in church polity and practice of the Roman church. Like Erasmus, he also stressed the necessity of a return to the biblical text, as opposed to relying on the church's tradition. Yet, and here lies the crucial difference between the two, for Luther the root of the problem with Rome is theological, and specifically, the doctrine of justification by faith, which for the reformer is inextricably linked with his understanding of the theology of the cross. In order to understand these truths properly, we need to understand humanity properly. To do that, we must address the issue of the will.

Erasmus's view of the will, according to Luther, cuts against the theology of the cross in two ways. First, it fails to consider the extent of corruption, sin, and wickedness that the cross portrays in humanity. In other words, the fact that Christ's death on the cross was required to pay for our sin reveals the great magnitude of our sin. A theology that fails to acknowledge utter human depravity, in Luther's view, diminishes the cross. Secondly, Luther's theology of the cross stands against human ability. The theology of glory looks to contribute to one's salvation; the theology of the cross looks to Christ alone in accomplishing it.

As Luther ends his treatise, he thanks Erasmus for downplaying trivial matters, such as the papacy, purgatory, and indulgences, but instead treating "the question upon which everything hinges," the question of the will. Consequently, debating Erasmus provided the opportunity to explore the centerpiece of the Reformation and the "vital spot" of a proper understanding of how one stands justified before God. Luther's treatise establishes two central points. First, the cross heralds both human sinfulness and human inability. Second, the cross also stresses God's majesty and grace. Luther's ruminations the day before his death give us the only possible conclusion to these two propositions: "We are beggars. That is true."

In reading Luther's *The Bondage of the Will,* we may not agree with all of his arguments, and admittedly some details are difficult to follow. Yet, his focus remains clear. He carefully stresses that we must articulate an understanding of salvation that does full justice to the biblical teaching involved and lets God be God. Certainly, we are left with questions concerning God's justice and human responsibility that we will probably fall short of satisfactorily resolving, even with Luther's help. His thought on this critical subject, nevertheless, helps us understand the fundamental truths of the issue. In one of his "Table Talk" selections, Luther concludes:

> Free will brought us sin and death. . . . Every part of us suffers corruption. So my position is this: Anyone who thinks that by free will he can do anything says "no" to

Christ. I have always taken this position in my writings, especially against Erasmus, one of the world's most learned scholars. I stand resolutely by my thesis because I know it is true. I will stand by it even if all the world opposes it. Divine truth stands. . . . You see then how different faith and free will really are. Free will equals nothing. Faith equals all that is good.

A Note on the Sources

As one of Luther's most well-known works, *The Bondage of the Will* has enjoyed numerous reprints and widespread attention. The full text, with a helpful introduction, may be found in *Luther's Works,* Volume 33. The complete text is also available, along with Erasmus's *On the Freedom of the Will: A Discourse,* in *Luther and Erasmus: Free Will and Salvation* (1969), edited by E. Gordon Rupp and Philip S. Watson. This text includes a helpful introduction. J. I. Packer and O. R. Johnston produced their own translation with a thorough introduction outlining Luther's life, the debate with Erasmus, and the primary themes of Luther's treatise in *The Bondage of the Will* (1957). Timothy F. Lull includes the introduction, the final section, and the conclusion in his *Martin Luther's Basic Theological Writings* (1989), pages 173–226. John Dillenberger offers portions of the text in *Martin Luther: Selections from His Writings* (1962), pages 166–203.

6

THIS IS MY BODY

Confession Concerning Christ's Supper

*"The Lord's Supper is given as a daily food and sustenance
so that our faith may refresh and strengthen itself and not
weaken in the struggle but continually grow stronger."*
Martin Luther, 1529

PHILLIP OF HESSE summoned an impressive gathering of theologians to his castle at Marburg in early October 1529. He, along with the other German and Swiss princes and rulers, faced three enemies: France, from the West; the Islamic forces or "Turks," from the East; and the Pope, ubiquitously. The princes could not afford to be divided; their lives and the survival of their provinces demanded a united front among the splintered reform movements to withstand these enemies at the gate. Luther was ambivalent toward the political issues, if not altogether averse to them. Yet, he was not content to pass on an occasion for a good theological debate. This engagement was what he longed for but never got with Rome. A serious

debate, with the best minds tackling the issues in an open setting—Luther dreamt of such things. Not surprisingly then,
he accepted Phillip's invitation and traveled to Marburg.

Theologians from the major cities comprising the Swiss
confederacy were present: John Oecolampadius, whose Latin
name means "house lamp," from Basel; Martin Bucer, a close
associate of Calvin's, from Strassburg; and Ulrich Zwingli,
father of the Swiss Reformation, from Zurich. Phillip, in
whose territory Marburg stands, provided an armor guard
ensuring safe travel and enabling Luther to attend, despite
the ban. In fact, the Marburg Colloquy was one of the few
meetings that he attended outside of Frederick's region.
Luther was joined by Justas Jonas and Philip Melanchthon
as representatives of Wittenberg. The other German prin-
cipalities were represented by Andreas Osiander, Stephen
Agricola, and Joannes Brentius. The two main characters in
this unfolding drama, however, were Luther and Zwingli.
Though Zwingli reached his conclusions regarding Rome's
errors independently from Luther's thought, he, nevertheless, had great admiration for the German reformer and
learned much from his writings.

The Marburg Colloquy, or formal meeting, lasted four
days. The parties discussed fifteen articles, and all agreed on
the first fourteen. But then sharp disagreement arose over
the last article, which concerned the Lord's Supper. Luther,
along with Melanchthon and the other German representatives, took the position that the "is" in "This *is* my body"
should be taken literally. They disagreed with the Catholic
position, which held that the elements, upon the priest's pro-
nouncement, transformed into the literal body and blood of
Christ. Luther dismissed such a view as nothing short of a
magic trick. In fact, the mass may very well be the source
of the term "hocus pocus." The Latin phrase for "This is my
body" is *Hoc est corpus meum*. An illiterate medieval auditor

altered *Hoc est corpus* to *hocus pocus,* a nonsense formula used by magicians to perform tricks and transform objects.

While disagreeing with the Catholic view, Luther, nevertheless, took these words seriously. For him, it was a matter of submitting to the text. This is not a prophetic or apocalyptic portion of Scripture that may have a figurative meaning. It is straightforward prose and should be taken literally. Theologians and historians often describe Luther's view as *consubstantiation.* This means that Christ, in substance, is with (from the Latin prefix *con)* the elements. This view stands opposed to the Catholic view designated *transubstantiation,* where the elements change, from the Latin prefix *trans,* to the very body or blood of Christ. Luther himself, however, never used this term to describe his view. It appears in the 1550s as a designation of his view by those who opposed it. The word consubstantiation reflects more philosophical speculation than Luther would accept. As we saw earlier, Luther tried to avoid such philosophical constructs in his theology. He preferred, instead, the label "real presence," or the "unity of the *sacrament."* He used this term to signify that Christ is in, with, and around the elements. Consequently, the communicant receives Christ's true body and blood, given for his sins.

Zwingli disagreed; he interpreted the "is" as "represents." Thus, he understood the elements in a memorial sense, as symbols pointing to the atoning work of Christ. To classify Zwingli's view of communion as a mere memorial, though, may not fully reflect his position. The crucial word for Zwingli is *contemplation.* He wrote that the communicant should so contemplate the mystery of Christ's redemptive work that one could "grasp the thing itself." He could not, however, follow Luther. Martin Bucer was on the fence theologically. He could not agree with Luther's view and was not entirely comfortable with Zwingli's understanding of communion, either. In short, the parties could not agree, and Philip's hopes of a united front among the reformers vanished as they all rode away from Marburg.

One might ask why the Reformation movement in Europe fragmented over the issue of the Lord's Supper and the little phrase, "This is my body." To understand the answer, we need to look closely at Luther's relevant thoughts.

Luther's Context: Trembling at His First Mass

We may well remember the poignant moment in Luther's early life and his spiritual struggles, described earlier, when he stood as a priest before the altar to perform his first mass. As he recited the words, "To you, the Eternal, Living, True God," Luther could barely stand on his trembling knees and strained to get the words out. These words, facilely spoken by the other priests, struck horror in Luther's soul. How could he approach this God? Even more pressing, how could Luther ever find forgiveness from such a God whom he had so violently offended? He found the answer in what the mass theoretically celebrated, the death of Christ on the cross. Little wonder, then, that the issue of the Lord's Supper occupied so much of Luther's attention.

Among the sacraments, this particular one took the lion's share of his interest. Many of his early works, from the time of the *Ninety-Five Theses* to the writing of *The Babylonian Captivity of the Church,* deal with this issue in a polemical fashion against Rome. Once Luther's break with Rome was finalized in 1521, he continued writing on the Lord's Supper in the same fashion. He shifted his focus, however, from Rome to the "fanatics," the Anabaptists, and to the Zwinglians, those who often abused Reformation principles and took Luther's ideas to an extreme. Between the years 1525–1529 especially, Luther and Zwingli engaged in a pamphlet and book war, which culminated in the gathering at Marburg. Luther's major contribution in all of this debate came in 1528, with the publication of *Confession Concerning Christ's Supper*. This work, which came after a tumultuous year for Luther, his family, and even the town of Wittenberg, because of illness and the plague, offers his most thorough discussion of the issue.

Confession Concerning Christ's Supper

Luther's work, *Confession Concerning Christ's Supper,* largely aims at responding to books by Zwingli and John Oecolampadius. In fact, Luther divides the book into three parts, devoting the first part to an elaborate criticism of their view. He primarily addresses the fundamental issue: How is one to interpret the "is" in "This *is* my body"? Luther clearly acknowledges that metaphors are used in Scripture. But, he adds "is" is never used to mean "represents." Luther thinks this is true even in ordinary grammar, apart from the literature of the Bible. He offers the expression "The monks are Pharisees," to prove his point. The best way to understand this saying is not to interpret it as meaning the monks represent Pharisees. Rather, the monks are "the new essence" of the Pharisees. (He appeals to the Roman poet, Horace, who says we use old words, Pharisees in this case, to coin a new understanding of new words, monks, in this case.)

He also sees a much wider application of Zwingli's understanding of "is" as "signifies." Earlier in "The Adoration of the Sacrament" (1523), he writes, "For if we permit such violence to be done in one passage, that without any basis in Scripture a person can say the word 'is' means the same as the word 'signifies,' then it would be impossible to stop it in any other passage." He adds there is nothing stopping

Fig. 6.1 Major Writings on the Lord's Supper and Related Events

May 2, 1507	Luther performs first Mass at his ordination
1519	Writes *The Blessed Sacrament of the Holy and True Body and Blood of Christ*
1520	Writes *The Babylonian Captivity of the Church*
Dec. 15, 1521	The church at Wittenberg administers Lord's Supper in "both kinds" (bread and cup) for the first time
1522	Writes *Receiving Both Kinds in the Sacrament*
1526	Writes *The Sacrament of the Body and Blood of Christ—Against the Fanatics*
1527	Writes *"This Is My Body"*
1528	Writes *Confession Concerning Christ's Supper*
Oct. 1-4, 1529	Marburg Colloquy takes place

one from claiming that the phrase "Christ is God and man," means that "Christ signifies God and man." Now, of course, Zwingli would refute this implication. And, perhaps, Luther's logic is not the tightest in this argument; it demonstrates, however, why Luther viewed this subject as essential.

Returning to *Confession Concerning Christ's Supper:* Luther next looks to Christ's sayings to understand better the use of the word "is." One such instance is John 15:1, "Christ is a true vine." Now this apparent use of a metaphor seems to favor Zwingli's view. Luther, however, observes that to say this means "Christ signifies the true vine" does not make much sense. As he asks rhetorically, "Do I hear correctly that Christ shall be a sign or symbol of the wood in the vineyard?" Luther concludes, "Hence the text irresistibly compels us to regard 'vine' as a new word, meaning a second, new, real vine, and not the vine in the vineyard." Luther then applies this principle to Christ's words concerning the bread and the cup. Consequently, according to Luther, the elements do not represent Christ, but the elements are the essence and nature of Christ's body which was given for us on the cross. This understanding does not mean that Christ reenacts the atonement at every communion. The issue of communion concerns the distribution of God's forgiveness, not the accomplishment of it. Luther puts the matter this way: "Christ has once for all merited and won forgiveness of sins on the cross; but this forgiveness he distributes wherever he is." And, Luther adds, he is in the elements. This conviction distinguishes Luther's view from that of Catholicism, which sees the atonement reenacted in the mass, and that of Zwinglianism, which pulls back from seeing the sacraments as a distribution of grace.

Throughout this first section of the book, Luther resists the urge to argue by way of philosophical speculation. The scholastic tradition, from which developed the Catholic view of transubstantiation, cast the discussions around sophisticated notions of substance. Luther avoided this approach altogether, arguing that he arrived at his view based on the promise of the sacrament. Zwingli often accused Luther of basing his view on philosophical speculation. Not surprisingly, Luther returned the same charge to Zwingli. In the final analysis, however, Luther reports that whatever problems may arise because of his view of the "real presence," he could not resolve them by recourse to philosophical speculation. Instead, he accepted it by faith, acknowledging that communion presents a profound mystery. As he writes early in 1525, in a response to Andreas Karlstadt and the fanatics, "How Christ is brought into the bread I do not know. But I know full well that the Word of God cannot lie, and it says that the body and blood of Christ are in the sacrament." Calvin did not attend the Marburg Colloquy, although the discussion greatly interested him. He actually said that he wished he could have been there, as he advocates a mediating position, sometimes referred to as the "spiritual presence" view. This view, according to Calvin, captures the strength of both Luther's and Zwingli's positions, while avoiding their pitfalls. Yet, Calvin concluded that he was closer to Luther's position than to Zwingli's.

Beyond the "real presence" view also stands Luther's understanding of the sacrament as a means of grace. By this, Luther meant that the sacraments of the Lord's Supper and baptism are other forms of the gospel. Superficially, this view seems to conflict with his understanding of the doctrine of justification and sounds as if he views salvation more as a process than an event. Perhaps, one of the statements from the fifteenth article of the Marburg Colloquy clarifies the matter. We recall that the fifteenth article was the source of disagreement between Luther and Zwingli. The article contains six separate statements. The last one, concerning the real presence of Christ in the elements, caused the division. The parties agreed, however, on the first five statements, which included this one: "As to the use of the sacrament, that like the Word of God Almighty, it has been given and ordained, in order that weak consciences might be excited by the Holy Ghost to faith and love." By designating the Lord's Supper as a means of grace, Luther intends to express God's gracious condescension in becoming sin for us, accomplished on the cross and distributed in communion.

In Part 2 of the book, he gives a detailed exposition on the various passages related to the Lord's Supper. Luther offers nothing original in this section, only turning to these passages to confirm his interpretation of "This is my body," and to substantiate his understanding of the Lord's Supper. In the final part of the book, Luther spends significant time clarifying his view and distinguishing it from opposing ones, all attempting to avoid any possible misuse of his ideas. Luther had learned a thing or two from his various theological tangos, and he applied that knowledge to this

HVLRICVS ZVINGLIVS.
Dicitur Hulricus se deuouisse duobus?,
Nempe Deo in primis, deinde etiam patriæ.
Quàm bene persoluit simul istis vota duobus,
Pro patria examinis, pro pietate cinis?
Cum priuill.

6.2 Portrait of Ulrich Zwingli, the Swiss reformer who found himself at odds with Martin Luther over the Lord's Supper.

situation at hand. He also uses the platform provided by the communion controversy to present his entire system of doctrine, including that which he affirmed and that which he renounced. Consequently, these last pages of *Confession Concerning Christ's Supper* become a concise statement of his doctrine. He begins this section with the words, "Hence lest any persons during my lifetime or after my death appeal to me or misuse my writings to confirm their error, as the sacramentarian and anabaptist fanatics are already beginning to do, I desire with this treatise to confess my faith before God and all the world, point by point." He devotes the least space to the Lord's Supper, primarily because the first two parts of the treatise so thoroughly engaged the issue.

A Solemn Occasion

Luther offered a succinct statement on the Lord's Supper in *The Small Catechism*. In a relatively brief series of five questions and answers, Luther explains "in plain form" what the "head of the family shall teach his household." He first defines the Lord's Supper, the "Sacrament of the Altar," as that which is instituted by Christ. He then presents the real presence view, explaining that the Lord's Supper "is the true body and blood of our Lord Jesus Christ, under the bread and wine, given to us Christians to eat." The second question concerns the biblical teaching for the Lord's Supper. In answering, he offers a series of quotations of both the synoptic gospel accounts and Paul's account of communion (1 Cor. 11:23–25; Matt. 26:26–28; Mark 14:22–24; and Luke 22:19–20). Having established his understanding of—and the biblical basis for—the Lord's Supper, Luther next explains the importance of the sacrament for the Christian life in the remaining three questions and answers.

The third question asks, "What is the benefit of such eating and drinking?" The answer reflects Luther's view of the sacrament as a means of grace. He states, "We are told in the words 'for you' and 'for the forgiveness of sins.' By these words the forgiveness of sins, life, and salvation, are given to us in the sacrament, for where there is forgiveness of sins, there are also life and salvation." He clarifies his point in the next question, and his answer stresses that it is not the elements, nor even the act of taking the elements, that "produce such great effects." Rather, as we have seen, it is the word of promise and belief in what these words declare. So the answer professes, "He who believes these words ['for you' and 'for forgiveness of sins'] has what they say and declare: the forgiveness of sins."

The final question and answer concerning the Lord's Supper address "preparation" and Paul's injunction concerning self-examination in 1 Corinthians 11:27–29. Paul refers to fasting as a "good external discipline" that prepares one for communion, but notes that the one who "is truly worthy and well prepared" is the one who believes in the promise of the sacrament. The one who "does not believe these words, or doubts them, is unworthy and unprepared, for the words 'for you' require truly believing hearts."

In *The Large Catechism*, Luther answers, in great detail, the question of self-examination and one's worthiness. In fact, he addresses this concern directly, raising a potential question in his reader as he writes, "But suppose you say, 'What if I feel that I am unfit?' " He first identifies with the question, noting, "This also is my temptation." He then offers a helpful perspective. Just because, he notes, we "are weak and frail," does not mean that we should refrain. "People with such misgivings must learn that it is the highest wisdom to realize that this sacrament does not depend upon our worthiness. . . . We come as poor, miserable men, precisely because we are unworthy." We should be compelled to come to the table of the Lord's Supper "by our own need, which hangs around our neck," not be deterred because of it.

Curiously, although it was for quite different reasons than for Luther, the Lord's Supper also became a point of controversy for Jonathan Edwards. A dispute between

Edwards and his Northampton congregation over admission to the Lord's Supper led to his dismissal in 1750. Although other issues were involved, mostly of a political nature in Edwards's case, nevertheless, communion was the one over which he was voted out. As the break between Luther and Zwingli, as well as the failure to mount a united front among the reformers because of differences over communion surprises us, so, too, Edwards's dismissal over the same concern might surprise as well. Our lack of considering different communion views as so essential might spring from the way this sacrament or ordinance has been marginalized in the contemporary church. A quick survey of church history reveals the centrality of the Lord's Supper at virtually every stage. And, returning to the pages of Acts reveals an equally prominent role for this sacrament at the very beginning of the church.

Today, communion does not always mean what it used to mean—or what it should mean. For some people, it undoubtedly remains a solemn occasion, cherished and held in reverence and viewed as an essential component to living the Christian life. For others, it may be more on the periphery, and for others still, it may be a discipline performed in a perfunctory manner, with little understanding of its true nature and little appreciation for its value. Luther's view of the Lord's Supper, even though not held by the majority of evangelicals, stands as a corrective to the shortcomings of our day. We may not agree with the real presence view, and some may even pull back from his discussion of the Lord's Supper as a means of grace. Nevertheless, the centrality that Luther affords it and the solemnity by which he approaches it provide a challenge to us today. As he reminds us in the words of *The Large Catechism*, the Lord's Supper is the food of the soul that nourishes and strengthens the new man. He continues, offering helpful words to contemplate the meaning and importance of the Lord's Supper the next time the communion elements are distributed:

> The Lord's Supper is given as a daily food and sustenance so that our faith may refresh and strengthen itself and not weaken in the struggle but continually grow stronger. . . . The devil is a furious enemy; when he sees that we resist him and attacks the old man, and when he cannot rout us by force, he sneaks and skulks about everywhere, trying all kinds of tricks, and does not stop until he has finally worn us out so that we either renounce our faith or yield hand and foot and become indifferent and impatient. For such times, when our heart feels too sorely pressed, this comfort of the Lord's Supper is given to bring us new strength and refreshment.

The practice of the Lord's Supper in contemporary Lutheran churches well attests to Luther's teaching on the solemnity of this discipline. The Lord's Supper was, for Luther, a serious occasion that impressed upon him the death of Christ and the need for faith in that work. Each time Luther partook of the sacrament he again met God on the cross, as Christ pays for his sins and secures his redemption from sin, death, and the devil. And here, as food nourishes the body, he found food for the soul and nourishment for living the Christian life.

A Note on the Sources

Since the Lord's Supper played a prominent role in Luther's thought, the subject pervades his writings. The three volumes specifically dedicated to the essential texts on the issue in *Luther's Works* are: *Volumes 35–37, Word and Sacrament I–III. Confession Concerning Christ's Supper* appears in Volume 37, 151–372, along with a helpful introduction by Robert H. Fischer. Timothy Lull includes a number of selections addressing the issue, including Part III of *Confession Concerning Christ's Supper* in *Martin Luther's Basic Theological Writings* (1989), pages 375–404.

7

PLAGUES, PRINCES, AND PEASANTS

Ethical Writings

*"Godliness is nothing else but service to God. Service
to God is indeed service to our neighbor."*
Martin Luther, 1527

T HE POLITICAL WORLD in which Luther lived is quite
different from that of the modern world. Church and
state, or empire, were so intertwined that one could
scarcely tell the difference between the two. Since 312 and the
reported conversion of Constantine at the Battle of Mulvian
Bridge, the church wrestled with its growing popularity and
favored status within the empire. In Constantine's day, he
held the power. A strong papacy had yet to emerge, and
the church was governed mostly by the bishops. Following
the collapse of the Roman Empire a century later, however,
the papal office rose first in ecclesiastical power, and then
in political power. As mentioned earlier, the crowning of

Charlemagne by Pope Leo III on Christmas Day, 800, signifies the extent of the power of the church, as Charlemagne received the crown from the pope's hands.

This strong relationship of church and state drifted far from Augustine's teaching on the issue in his work *The City of God*. His book came largely as an apologetic to the charge that the Christians were responsible for the demise of the Roman Empire. Augustine started writing the work in 413 as just that. By the time he finished in 426, he had accomplished much more. Among the many things covered in the book is the distinction between the two cities: the earthly city, the City of Man, and the heavenly city, the City of God. He further viewed these two cities in locked conflict. The ultimate victor, of course, was the City of God. A Chris-tian's ultimate allegiance was there also. We'll see shortly, as Luther engages this model, that perhaps Augustine overstated the matter of the Christian's disinterest in the earthly city. Nevertheless, he set up distinct boundaries between these two cities. Over the following centuries, however, those distinctions became increasingly blurred until the two cities eventually merged.

Historians refer to this dynamic as the "medieval synthesis," or the bringing together of all of life under the sphere of the church. It is also known as Christendom, the world into which Luther was born. But, just as Luther's ideas changed both the theological and ecclesiastical world, his ideas helped shape a new social and political landscape.

The Two Kingdoms and the Three Estates

Luther would admit freely that the papacy and the church had overstepped its bounds. As we saw in his *Address to the German Nobility,* Luther challenged the Roman church's assertion of power over the German princes. While Luther held to a certain separation of church and state, he also distanced

Fig. 7.1 Major Ethical Writings

1519	"A Sermon on the Estate of Marriage"
1520	*To the Christian Nobility of the German Nation (Three Treatises)*
1522	*The Estate of Marriage*
1523	*On Temporal Authority: To What Extent Should It Be Obeyed*
April 1525	*Admonition to Peace Based on the Twelve Articles of the Peasants in Swabia*
May 1525	*Against the Robbing and Murdering Bands of Peasants*
July 1525	*An Open Letter on the Harsh Book Against the Peasants*
1527	*Whether One May Flee from a Deadly Plague*
1531	*Dr. Martin Luther's Warning to His Dear German People*

himself from the radical wing of the Reformation. Historians designate the various Anabaptist groups as comprising the radical Reformation not because of our understanding of the term radical, but because the Latin word, *radix,* from which we get the English word radical means "root." The radical reformers wanted to go further than Luther, Zwingli, and Calvin and get at the root of the problem: the merger of church and state. Consequently, the radical reformers advocated a total separation of church and state, a mark of Anabaptist traditions that continues to this day. It was an idea, however, that Luther could not see as right. He forged his own way, and, in the process, developed a significant understanding of how to relate these two spheres of the church and state.

Borrowing from Augustine, Luther viewed the two cities as two kingdoms in conflict. And, he held that the Kingdom of God will prevail. Unlike Augustine and the radical reformers, Luther saw value in the earthly kingdom. The Christian, he argued, is a citizen of both kingdoms, liable to their laws and customs and participant in the activities of each. Further,

God's law concerns both kingdoms. Luther demonstrates this by appealing to the essence of the law, as summarized by Christ. The first great commandment, to love God with one's whole heart, soul, mind, and strength, concerns the kingdom of God. The second, to love one's neighbor, governs the Christian's life in the earthly kingdom (Luke 10:27). The Christian should also not preclude the earthly kingdom because it was created by God. In fact, Luther refers to Augustine's city of humanity as the kingdom of creation. He also prefers the term "kingdom of redemption" to the designation of the city of God.

These two kingdoms, the kingdom of creation and the kingdom of redemption, function separately, and, to be sure, the kingdom of redemption takes priority ultimately and in the individual's life. The Christian, however, is to live as a citizen of both, and Luther argues that God does not leave us without some instructions as to how to be good citizens of both. The summation of the law as both to love God and to love our neighbor is a good place to start. Luther, like so many others, however, sees this representing the so-called two tables of the law. Consequently, he sees the first five commandments of the Ten Commandments as governing one's relationship to God, while he views the second five as directing one's relationship to his or her neighbor (Ex. 20). In Luther's view, God created this world, and he placed us in it for a reason. He commanded us to care for it, and he has shown us how he would have us live in it. We, as citizens of the kingdom of redemption, nevertheless, remain citizens of the kingdom of creation. We live, as it were, with our feet in both worlds.

There is another layer to Luther's understanding of the Christian's relation to society which concerns his notion of the three estates. The three estates reflect the God-given order or hierarchy in the world. They also govern our various relationships in the world, preserving the kingdom of creation. Here Luther helpfully advances Augustine's thought on the Christian's relationship to the world. His teaching on the three estates permeates his writings. Perhaps his most succinct treatment comes in his *Confession Concerning Christ's Supper* (1528). Here he writes, "But the holy orders and true religious institutions established by God are these three estates: the office of the priest, marriage, and the civil government." The first estate, the "priestly estate," obviously entails those who preach the word and administer the sacrament. Luther sees the office as ordained by God to promulgate the gospel, admonish, and instruct. The second estate concerns the "domestic sphere," involving not only husbands and wives, but parents and children, as well as widows and singles. Here, Luther argues that "those who regulate their household wisely and bring up their children to the service of God are engaged in pure holiness, in a holy work and a holy order." By using the word "order" Luther fully lodges a criticism against what he refers to as the "false institution" of monasticism and its orders.

Finally, he addresses the "temporal estate," which entails ruling authorities and their subjects. He explains that the members of this estate "are all engaged in pure holiness and leading a holy life before God." In 1523, Luther devoted an entire treatise, *On Temporal Authority: To What Extent It Should Be Obeyed,* to this estate. He adds one more estate:

> Above these three institutions and orders is the common order of Christian love, in which one serves not only the three orders, but also serves every needy person in general with all kinds of benevolent deeds, such as feeding the hungry, giving drink to the thirsty, forgiving enemies, praying for all men on earth, suffering all kinds of evil on earth, etc. Behold, all of these are called good and holy works.

Ob man sur dem sterben fliehen muge.
Mart. Luther
Wittemberg.
M. D. XXVII.

7.2 Title page for Luther's pamphlet, *Whether One May Flee from a Deadly Plague*, one of his many ethical writings.

As he explains, however, while these estates are "holy works," they do not bring about salvation, neither do they necessarily concern salvation. He adds, "None of these orders is a means of salvation. There remains only one way above them all, faith in Christ Jesus. For to be holy and to be saved are two different things. . . . Even the godless may have much about them that is holy without being saved." Luther's thoughts here need some explanation. Differentiating what these estates accomplish from that which salvation accomplishes fits well with Luther's two-kingdom idea. Salvation belongs to the kingdom of redemption, while these estates belong to the kingdom of creation. What often confuses us is Luther's use of the word "holy." We might prefer to say morality, instead. Yet, Luther's designation of these estates as holy, even though they are earthly and do not necessarily lead to salvation, demonstrates the importance he attaches to our life in the kingdom of creation.

Putting the two kingdoms and the three estates together, we can see Luther's advice for life in the kingdom of creation. First, we must realize that there is conflict between these two kingdoms. This world, though created by God, nevertheless is "with devils filled." Second, Luther reminds us that despite the conflict, again borrowing a phrase from "A Mighty Fortress," God's "kingdom is forever." In other words, the kingdom of redemption ultimately triumphs. So far, Luther follows Augustine. He adds, however, that we are also citizens of the kingdom of creation. Firstly, God created it; secondly, God commands us to be responsible citizens, which in some way lends credence to it, and thirdly, we are to care for our neighbor as we live in it. Finally, God instituted the three estates to preserve creation. Against Augustine, who largely viewed the two kingdoms as in conflict, and against the medieval view, which confused the two kingdoms, Luther advocates that citizens of the kingdom of redemption make meaningful contributions to the kingdom of creation.

Luther's understanding of the two kingdoms and the three estates provides the basis for his social ethics. From this foundation he approaches numerous ethical quandaries. His life provided him with no shortage of opportunities to put his ethics into practice. Below we will look at two specific issues that tested Luther and his ideas. First, the plague not only struck his hometown of Wittenberg, but also took the lives of his relatives and close friends. This trial tested Luther's commitment to the command to love one's neighbor. Second, the Peasants' War challenged Luther and his understanding of the relationship between church and state and of social ethics. It also provided a platform for him to address the relationship to temporal authorities. We will look at these issues shortly to see Luther's ethics and how he applied them.

The Plague

Luther lived out his ethic, and he did so at considerable personal risk. His challenge to the status quo and his courage to live out his convictions put him at odds with those in power over him. It brought him under the ban and led to his being declared an outlaw. Additionally, Luther and his family lived through a time of tremendous upheaval during the Peasants' War, a subject which we will address soon. Luther and his family also endured great personal sacrifice and tremendous risk by converting their home's living quarters and lecture rooms at the Black Cloister into a hospital during the plague in 1527. This year was exceptionally difficult for the family. Luther suffered such a serious illness that he thought he never would recover from it. The Luthers' only son, Hans, just one year old, also became seriously ill. Meanwhile Katie was expecting their second child, who would be born that December. In addition, Luther continued to be occupied with a number of controversies, including the communion controversy with Zwingli. And in July of that year the plague hit Wittenberg.

Life was so difficult that John Frederick, the nephew

of Frederick the Wise, who ruled Saxony after his uncle's death in 1525, ordered the faculty and students of the university to move to the city of Jena. Martin Luther defied his order. He was also joined by another faculty member, Johannes Bugenhagen. Bugenhagen, a gifted linguist and biblical scholar, was won to Luther's views by reading *The Babylonian Captivity of the Church*. He also served as a primary committee member for Luther's translation of the Old Testament. He remained one of Luther's closest and most faithful supporters, and during this time of trial he chose to stay with his mentor. Bugenhagen was also mourning his wife's death, a victim of the plague. Luther, in addition to being the venerable doctor of theology, also, for a time, tried standing in as a medical doctor and cared for the sick and dying in his home. Eventually, the plague subsided, but not before it took eighteen lives, many of whom died in Luther's home. By November, life in the town of Wittenberg returned to normal. The students and faculty of the university did not return, however, until April of the following year.

While the plague struck Wittenberg, it also devastated other cities, including Breslau. One of the pastors there wrote Luther for advice on whether one should flee cities hit by the plague. Luther was simply too busy to reply until November. When he did, he sent an open letter, which was widely distributed, entitled "Whether One May Flee from a Deadly Plague." In the letter, Luther offers sound advice, but he avoids a simple answer. Rather, his thoughts reveal the issue's complexity. He begins by noting that "some people are of the firm opinion that one need not and should not run away from a deadly plague. Instead, since death is God's punishment, which he sends upon us for our sins, we must submit to God and with a true and firm faith patiently await our punishment." Luther acknowledges that such a position evidences a "strong faith" and "deserves commendation."

Yet, he cautions against such a position. First, he observes that while few Christians are strong, "many are weak." Consequently, "one cannot simply place the same burden on everyone." Secondly, as he develops this point later, this may not entirely represent the true life of faith.

Once Luther confronts the conventional wisdom, he offers his reply. While he stresses that the laity, or the common people, may flee, he is not so flexible when it comes to pastors and governmental authorities. He advises that pastors "should remain steadfast before the peril of death." "For when people are dying," he reasons, "they most need a spiritual ministry which strengthens and comforts their consciences." He adds, however, that if there are enough ministers to serve, then they can agree among themselves who goes and who stays. He similarly advises that "all those in public office such as mayors, judges, and the like are under obligation to remain." He points out that "to abandon an entire community which has been called [by God] to govern and to leave it without official or government, exposed to all kinds of danger such as fires, murder, riots, and every imaginable disaster is a great sin." Luther consistently applied his understanding of both the God-given and necessary role of government to maintain order, especially in times of crisis.

Other groups are also duty-bound; Luther concludes that servants should not leave without their master's consent and then quickly adds that the reverse is true as well. So it is with parents to children, and the reverse. Luther also admonishes that orphans be cared for. And, then he turns to one's duty as a neighbor. Loving one's neighbor, as we have seen, is Luther's fundamental social ethic. Here he reveals that lip service to this principle simply will not do: "No one should dare leave his neighbor unless there are others who will take care of the sick. . . . In such cases we must respect the words of Christ, 'I was sick and you did not visit me.' " According to this passage we are bound to each other in such a way that no one may forsake the other in his distress. Luther returns to this point later in the letter. At this juncture, however, he pauses to stress that if enough remain to care for the sick, then those who can should flee. He observes that we "should seek to preserve life and avoid death."

Luther also advocated a common sense approach as opposed to an abuse of faith. Instead of a cavalier attitude toward the plague, Luther advised, "Use medicine; take potions which can help you; fumigate house, yard, and street; shun persons and places wherever your neighbor does not need your presence or has recovered." Luther himself quarantined his house after it had served as a hospital during the plague, just to be cautious. The underlying principle, however, is to love one's neighbor. For Luther, this was not only applied in the best of times, but also in the worst. He stated, "A man who will not help or support others unless he can do so without affecting his safety or his property will never help his neighbor." He adds, "Godliness is nothing else but service to God. Service to God is indeed service to our neighbor." Luther tried to live by all of these principles that he publicly expressed. He took precaution, not abusing faith, but he also served his neighbor boldly and at great personal risk.

Princes and Peasants

The Peasants' War also presented an ethical challenge to Luther. He had a complex relationship with the peasants. From the time that the *Ninety-Five Theses* were translated into German and widely circulated, the peasants heralded Luther as a hero. At first he applauded and even encouraged their efforts at political reform. Consequently, when he vehemently spoke out against the excesses of the peasants' revolt, they initially expressed confusion which quickly dissolved into anger and animosity.

The German peasants in the 1520s lived under the feudal system, which usually favored the wealthy landowners at the expense of the poorer class. The landowners, who made the laws and governed, naturally instituted laws and handed down rulings that favored their own agenda. At times the system grew oppressive, even cruel. The peasants had little in their favor, but they had large numbers. Spurred on by Luther's writings, such as the *Ninety-Five Theses* and *The Freedom of the Christian,* as well as his challenge to the oppressive ecclesiastical structure, the peasants were inspired to mount a challenge to the political and economic structures bequeathed from the medieval period. Luther did not approve of the distortion of his ideas to substantiate the cause. Nevertheless, he identified with the peasants, seeing them as an oppressed group who were unfairly treated. He also cautioned them to seek change properly, to avoid violence, plundering, and murder. Tragically, the movement grew out of control and did exactly as Luther warned against, with devastating results.

The war's first skirmish came in 1524 when a countess near the Black Forest ordered her peasants, during the middle of their harvest time, to stop their labors and pick berries for her. They needed their crop not only to provide for their own food, but also to pay the high fees that were extracted from them for the privilege of farming their lord's lands. Before long, a small army of peasants numbering just over one thousand formed and rebelled. Eventually, the numbers grew larger and the rebellions more common. By the spring of 1525, the insurrections escalated into a war. The nobility responded with horrific might, executing the leaders and killing thousands at the Battle of Frankenhausen in the early days of May 1525. Thomas Muenzer, originally an adherent to Luther's ideas and a pastor at Zwickau, was one of the main leaders. By 1520, he became a fanatic and an Anabaptist, the main figure in the group that Luther referred to as the "Zwickau prophets." He advocated the "inner light" as opposed to the Bible as the source of God's revelation. His inner light informed him to kill the godless nobles. When the peasants were defeated at Frankenhausen, he was beheaded.

Luther witnessed these events; he also tried to intervene. He aimed three writings in particular at events unfolding from April to July 1525. In the first piece, *Admonition to Peace Based on the Twelve Articles of the Peasants of Swabia,* he criticizes the princes and nobility for their callousness, excesses, and vanity. After a brief introduction, he addresses the princes, stating, "We have no one on earth to blame for this disastrous rebellion, except you princes and lords." He calls on them to take this rebellion seriously and to consider the peasants' reasonable demands. He exclaims, "These protests are right and just, for rulers are not appointed to exploit their subjects for their own profit and advantage, but to be concerned about the welfare of their subjects." Luther then addresses the peasants; in essence, he wanted them to be patient: "[B]e careful that you take up your cause justly and with a good conscience." He even refers to Muenzer, although not by name, as he writes, "Look carefully at what you are doing and do not believe all kinds of spirits and preachers." He further reminds the peasants of the biblical injunction to be submissive. He ends the treatise by predicting the outcome, even though he wishes that he could prevent it. He forewarns, "As I see it, the worst thing about this completely miserable affair is that both sides will sustain irreparable damage; and I would gladly risk my life and even die if I could to prevent that from happening."

Luther prophesied accurately; in response to the defeat in May, the peasants, never much of a unified army, made various attacks. Luther offered his *Against the Robbing and Murdering Bands of Peasants* in July of that same year. He addressed their "intolerable rebellion" as not only a sin against humanity, but an affront to God. Because of the bloodshed and pillaging caused by certain peasants, Luther expressed that the princes were just in responding with force. His advice, however, was taken too far by the princes, and their response extended even to those who were entirely innocent. Consequently, Luther offered one final installment on the affair entitled *An Open Letter on the Harsh Book Against the Peasants* in August. The "harsh book" was his own piece from July. Luther defended his ideas in both that book, as well as his first one, *Admonition to Peace*. He also, however, condemns those who abuse his ideas or cloak their own excesses in his ideas. He further uses the event to instruct both sides to be more conscious of a higher call than to be consumed by temporal cares: "We are acting as mad Germans always do: we know nothing about God, and we talk about these things as though there were no God who does them and wills them that they be done. We do not intend to suffer at all, but to be nobles, who can sit on cushions and do as they please."

In each of these writings, Luther attempted to let God and his Word inform these issues. He found that princes, or any authority, err when that authority is abused for personal gain over the interests of the common good. He also found that peasants, or any under authority, need to submit and to address grievances in a proper, patient way. In these writings, we also see his thoughts on conflict, a subject with which he was quite familiar. Luther didn't seek out conflict; nevertheless, it followed him at virtually every turn. Not only did he have his conflict with the pope and the church, but he also found himself in the center of conflict in 1525 and beyond. And, as with his treatment of the plague, he tried to respond by turning to the guiding principles of Scripture.

Luther on Ethics

It is unlikely that most of us will face a plague. Few of us will be "princes," and, perhaps, will never witness a revolution firsthand. Yet, this does not mean that Luther's thoughts are not applicable to us. The plague and the political turmoil of the 1520s and 1530s demanded a response from Luther and his contemporaries. Luther applied good theology to these crises, as he sought to ground his ethics and his understanding of politics and social philosophy on biblical bases. A remarkable quality in Luther's ethics concerns its timeliness and universality. As we read through Luther's ethical writings, we find elements that apply strictly to his situation in the first half of the sixteenth century. We also find, however, principles that transcend that time. Additionally, and perhaps most remarkably, Luther's ethics resound with pure simplicity. For Luther, the essence of all law—human or divine—governing our earthly life, or as he prefers, the kingdom of creation, is to love one's neighbor. This is a command which, he himself once confessed, provides enough material to last a lifetime.

Two years after the plague, Luther published the *Small Catechism*, containing these words: "We should fear and love God, and we should not endanger our neighbor's life, nor cause him any harm, but help and befriend him in every necessity of life." Remarkably, he not only wrote these words, he lived them.

A Note on the Sources

Four volumes are devoted to Luther's various ethical writings in *Luther's Works*. These include *Volumes 44–47, The Christian in Society I–IV*. Timothy Lull includes selections from ethical writings, including "Whether One May Flee from a Deadly Plague," in *Martin Luther's Basic Theological Writings* (1989), pages 577–755. John Dillenberger includes *Temporal Authority: To What Extent It Should Be Obeyed* in *Martin Luther: Selections from His Writings* (1962), pages 363–402.

PART THREE

LUTHER, THE PASTOR

L
UTHER'S PRIMARY DEVOTION was to the church. From the time he entered the monastery until his death—and at every point in between—Luther thought about, wrote on, preached to, and fought for the church. These next chapters explore just a sampling of Luther's contributions to church life. We begin with Luther's efforts in training up the next generation. The *Small Catechism*, a tool that Luther himself used quite frequently with his own children, remains an enduring legacy to Luther's concern for the church's theological well-being long after he passed from the scene. Luther frequently opened his home to his colleagues and the students at the university. These gatherings around the table after the evening meal reveal unprecedented glimpses into the personal side of Luther. They also show, by practice, Luther's commitment to discipleship and mentoring.

After theology, Luther's major passion was music. In chapter 10 we listen to Luther as he combines both of his passions and teaches theology through music. In many ways, the practice of worship and the role of music in our church services reflects Luther's legacy as his reforms extended to this vital activity of the church. *On the Councils and the Church,* the subject of chapter 11, takes up the crucial question of the marks of the true church. Finally, Luther typically preached five times a week and left behind some 6,000 sermon manuscripts. From among this immense sermon corpus, we examine one sermon in particular, "Contemplating Christ's Suffering." This sermon represents well his preaching and offers insight into what Luther's congregation at the Castle Church enjoyed on a regular basis.

8

THE NEXT GENERATION

The Small Catechism

*"I haven't yet progressed beyond the instruction of children in the
Ten Commandments, the Creed, and the Lord's Prayer. I still learn
and pray these everyday with my Hans and my little Lena."*
Martin Luther, 1531

MARTIN LUTHER was the quintessential busy pastor.
He performed multiple duties, including writing,
preaching, teaching, and administrating. In any
given week, he wrote numerous lengthy letters or worked on
one of his many treatises, preached two times on Sunday and
typically three more times during the week, lectured daily at
the university, mentored students, and advised any number
of fledgling pastors, churches, and even princes. In addition,
he tended to his ever expanding family. He also experienced
the strains that the various controversies placed on his time
and energy. Yet, in the midst of this constant activity, he
devoted hours to teaching not only his own children, but
the children of Wittenberg. Luther possessed an incredible

intellect. His translation of the Greek New Testament into German in merely three months stands as a clear testimony to his genius. He engaged in debate with the most brilliant minds of his day. Long before his notoriety spread with the posting of the *Ninety-Five Theses*, he had established himself clearly as one of Germany's most promising academics. And, perhaps the most telling mark of his intellectual prowess, he taught children the essential truths of the Christian faith in ways they could understand.

This emphasis on teaching children, which could have been very easily crowded out by other demands, made perfect sense to Martin Luther. For the fledgling church that soon came to bear his name, as well as the entire Protestant movement, not only to survive, but also to flourish, teaching children assumed a crucial, if not urgent priority. Luther knew this not only from historical examples, but from observing the present situation. Throughout the fall and winter months of 1528 and 1529, he toured the new congregations throughout the region. He was still an outlaw, so the tour was not without its risk. Yet, he traveled to see firsthand the condition of the churches. The results of the inspection left Luther frustrated and disappointed. He found conditions "deplorable" and "wretched" and added, "The common people, especially those who live in the country, have no knowledge whatsoever of Christian teaching, and unfortunately many pastors are incompetent and unfitted for teaching."

"They have mastered the fine art," Luther intoned, "of abusing liberty." This situation deeply troubled Luther. He focused his concerns on two groups, the clergy and the children. Upon returning to Wittenberg he immediately asked Melanchthon and the others from his circle of friends and colleagues to produce materials addressing these deficiencies and to train children. They produced reams of material, some of which he approved. Some of it he considered nothing more than moralism—a cure which he feared to be worse than the disease. But he perceived that virtually all of it fell short of accomplishing what he thought essential: the communication of the clear teaching of the central truths of the Bible and orthodox theology from one generation to the next. In other words, he desired an enduring tradition, in the best sense of the term.

The English word *tradition* derives directly from the Latin word *traditio*, which means to transfer, hand down, or give over. For Luther, Paul captured the meaning of the word best when he admonished his "son in the faith," Timothy, to hand down that which he had heard from him to faithful men, who will in turn be able to teach others (2 Tim. 2:2). Luther extrapolated from this the understanding of the only way for the church to remain faithful to the gospel and orthodox theology. It must teach—explicitly, purposefully, and programmatically—the gospel and orthodox theology, and it must do so to the young.

After waiting fruitlessly for someone else to write the material that would accomplish this, Luther decided to do it himself in 1529. The result is *The Small Catechism*. By his own testimony, as we have seen, Luther declared that he did not mind if all were burned and forgotten, as long as *The Bondage of the Will* and *The Small Catechism* survived. Thankfully, his wish came true without the condition. This work has survived and thrived. It continues to find a wide audience even now, nearly five hundred years after it was written. Luther also addressed the problems of unlearned clergy with the publication which he simply titled *The German Catechism* the same year. This work, which has come to be labeled *The Large Catechism*, follows the same structure as its smaller counterpart, only much more extensively.

The Small Catechism was not the only contribution that Luther made to children's literature. He also, as mentioned earlier, published a German translation of Aesop's Fables. In addition, he authored a simple alphabet and children's book. *The Small Catechism,* however, remains his true legacy and earns him yet another addition to his extensive list of credentials: child educator.

A Theological Masterpiece—for Children

The Small Catechism is a masterpiece in being both comprehensive and concise. Timeless in its presentation, style, and content, the work ranks among classics of both devotional and theological literature. It consists of a brief exposition of the essential elements in understanding God, his Word, and his work in the world, as it contains brief teachings on the Ten Commandments, the Apostle's Creed, the Lord's Prayer, and the sacraments. Luther expanded the catechism in later editions to include instructions on prayer and what he referred to as "the table of duties." These quite small entries present various teachings from the Bible concerning pastors, temporal authorities, husbands, wives, parents, children, laborers and servants, masters, and widows, and conclude with a word to all Christians generally. Luther's was the first of many catechisms produced during the Reformation, including the *Heidelberg Catechism* and the *Westminster Shorter* and *Larger Catechisms.*

Like these others, Luther's follows a question and answer model. The word *catechism* literally means to sound out and connotes teaching by way of speaking. The method of catechetical instruction emphasizes involvement of the teacher or parent and the child. It also encourages memorization, as the questions and answers are repeated frequently. The repetition and memorization, however, are means to an end, as the words of the catechism are to impact both the thinking and the life of the one who knows the words.

Catechisms were not an innovation in church practice by Luther. The medieval church used catechetical instruction, even structuring catechisms around the Ten Commandments, the Lord's Prayer, the Apostle's Creed, and the sacraments. What is unique to Luther's catechism is both the content and the audience for it. As Luther developed his expositions of the various elements of the catechism, he arrived at remarkably different conclusions than the medieval understanding. As for audience, the medieval catechisms largely aimed at adults, and even then only at a limited few. Luther targeted an entirely new audience, children, and he further hoped that the catechism would be enjoyed by all church members, not just a select few.

Indeed, his catechism reached and continues to reach a wide audience. It is probably Luther's most widely read work. It lacks the polemical elements that the wrangling with other thinkers brought out in much of his other writing. Additionally, it has an unmatched simplicity and clarity. Yet, it also has similarities with his other writings. The main ideas that he continually stressed appear throughout the catechism. In the pages that follow we will explore those themes as we learn from Luther the essentials of the Christian faith.

Christian Ethics: The Ten Commandments

Luther once remarked that "whoever knows well how to distinguish the gospel from the law should give thanks to God and know that he is a real theologian." In the catechism, Luther comes close to demonstrating that he meets his own criteria. The relationship between law and gospel receives extensive treatment in his thought. He begins with the law, the Decalogue, as offering a clear portrayal of both sin and grace. The law, according to Luther, is to convict and to show our sin. Further, the law accuses, even torments and horrifies us. Yet, in the midst of the law, grace abounds.

A definite pattern emerges from this catechism section that continues through the entire text. He cites the commandment, then asks simply, "What does this mean?" ("*Was ist das?*"). Admittedly, the repeating question lacks originality and variety. Whatever qualities may be lacking in the question, however, he supplies in the answer. Concerning the first commandment, "You shall have no other gods," Luther asks his trademark question, "What does this mean?" and then follows by answering, "We should fear, love, and trust God above all things." This tendency to pull a positive teaching from the negative command reverberates throughout his discussion of the Ten Commandments. In fact, he uses the first part of the answer to the question concerning the first commandment, "We should fear and love God," to begin the rest of the answers. Luther is guarding those children (and us) from simply viewing the Ten Commandments as an external law code. He also keeps us from moralism by grounding the basis and motive for adhering to the Ten Commandments in nothing other than an expression of grateful obedience to God. According to Luther, one's relationship to God grounds an obedient Christian life.

Consider his answer to the fifth commandment, "You shall not kill," as representative of his treatment of the other commandments. Here Luther informs us that "we should love and fear God, and we should not endanger our neighbor's life, nor cause him any harm, but help and befriend him in every necessity of life." In keeping with his teaching on social ethics, he appeals to Christ's summary of the law as to love God and to love one's neighbor as the orienting principle for his treatment of others. Keeping the commandment not to take the life of another probably does not present the large majority of us with much of a challenge. But, it is

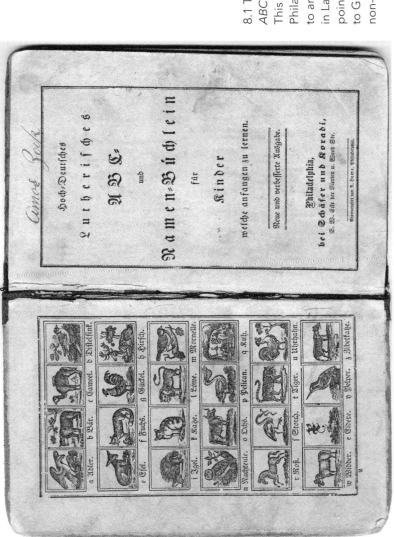

8.1 Title page of Luther's *ABC Book for Children.* This copy, published in Philadelphia, belonged to an Amish farmer in Lancaster, PA, and points to Luther's legacy to Germans—even non-Lutherans.

quite a challenge to keep the spirit of this law, and, as Luther expressed, help and befriend our neighbor in every necessity of life. Turning to the fourth commandment, we should not only keep from despising our parents, but "honor, love, serve, obey, and esteem them." We should not only refrain from bearing false witness as the eighth command requires, but also "apologize for him, speak well of him, and interpret charitably all that he does." And so he walks us through the Ten Commandments.

Once Luther treats each of the commandments, he concludes the first part of the catechism with a summary statement capturing well that connection of law and grace:

> God threatens to punish all who transgress these commandments. We should therefore fear his wrath and not disobey these commandments. On the other hand, he promises grace and every blessing to all who keep them. We should therefore love him, trust in him, and cheerfully do what he has commanded.

Christian Doctrine: The Apostle's Creed

Using the familiar words of the Apostle's Creed, Luther in the second part of the catechism explains basic doctrines concerning the persons and work of the Trinity. In unfolding the Creed, Luther groups the separate phrases of it around the three articles of creation, redemption, and sanctification. These three works reflect the particular involvement of the members of the Godhead, God the Father, the Son, and the Holy Spirit. Beginning with God as creator, Luther makes the broad and general opening statement of the creed, "I believe in God, the Father almighty, maker of heaven and earth," concrete and personal for his young listeners. To be sure, this means that God created the entire, vast universe and everything in it merely by his word. But what impresses Luther here is not so much this fact, but, "God created me and all that exists." He continues to exclaim that he believes that God "has given me and still sustains my body and soul, all my limbs and senses, my reason and all the faculties of my mind, together with food and clothing, house and home, family and property." God also "provides me daily and abundantly with all the necessities of life, protects me from all danger, and preserves me from all evil." All of this attests to God's "pure, fatherly, and divine goodness and mercy, without any merit or worthiness on my part." Consequently, according to Luther, only one response is adequate: "to thank, praise, serve, and obey him."

In the second article concerning redemption, Luther supplements the words of the Apostle's Creed in his answer by using phrases from the Nicene Creed. While the Apostle's Creed mentions the deity of Christ by referring to him as "our Lord," it does not do so emphatically. One can also infer Christ's humanity from other phrases of the creed, but again it lacks an emphatic statement concerning his humanity. Luther, borrowing from the Nicene Creed, makes these implicit teachings explicit in his answer by referring to Christ both as "true God" and "true man." The bulk of Luther's answer, however, expounds Christ's work of redemption on our behalf. This work, which "delivered me from all my sins, from death, and from the power of the devil," enables me "to live under him in his kingdom," and also challenges me "to serve him."

Reading this second part of the explanation of the Apostle's Creed on Christ's work of redemption in tandem with the catechism's teaching on the Ten Commandments reveals the connection between Christian ethics and doctrine. As Moses presents the Ten Commandments in Exodus 20, he points first to the exodus event and Israel's deliverance from slavery in Egypt. We could interpret this as meaning that because of what God has done for us, we should be obedient to him. Because Christ has redeemed us, we should live for and serve him. Doctrine leads to ethics. Richard Gaffin, a Westminster Theological Seminary professor, expresses the matter this way: the *imperatives* are based on the *indicatives*. He explains that as meaning the "imperatives" of the Ten Commandments or the "imperatives" of living the Christian life are based on the "indicatives," or what God has done in redeeming Israel out of Egypt and what he has done in redeeming us from sin.

Luther then turns his attention to the Holy Spirit's work and the believer's sanctification in the last article. His understanding of the Apostle's Creed's final phrases reveal that the Holy Spirit enables us to come to Christ. Not only has the Spirit "called me through the gospel," but he also "enlightened me with his gifts, and sanctified and preserved me in the true faith." This gift of the Spirit extends beyond me to the entire church, which he also sanctifies and preserves. Luther ends each of these three sections with the words, "This is most certainly true." Familiar words, like those of the Apostle's Creed, sometimes risk the danger of rote expression. Luther's parting words in explaining what the creed means remind us of the ultimate importance of these doctrines to our life.

Christian Practice: The Lord's Prayer, Sacraments, and Table of Duties

Luther next addresses the spiritual discipline of prayer by looking to Christ's words. He views prayer as an essential part of the Christian life in part simply because it was commanded by God. But, he also recognizes it as a necessary means to living the Christian life. In *The Large Catechism*,

Dr. Martin Luthers kleiner Katechismus

(1529)

Das erste Hauptstück

Die zehn Gebote

Das erste Gebot
Ich bin der Herr, dein Gott;
du sollst keine anderen Götter neben mir haben.

> **Was ist das?**
> Wir sollen Gott über alle Dinge fürchten, lieben und vertrauen.

Das zweite Gebot
Du sollst den Namen deines Gottes nicht mißbrauchen.

> **Was ist das?**
> Wir sollen Gott fürchten und lieben,
> daß wir bei seinem Namen nicht fluchen,
> schwören, zaubern, lügen oder trügen,
> sondern denselbigen in allen Nöten anrufen,
> beten, loben und danken.

8.2 The first page of a German text of Luther's *Small Catechism* contains the first two commandments. The repeated question, "Was ist das?" or "What does this mean?" appears throughout the work.

he explains how this is so, observing, "Nothing is so necessary as to call upon God incessantly and drum into his ears our prayer that he may give, preserve, and increase in us faith and obedience." Prayer also causes us to reflect on our needs. "Each of us," Luther exhorts, "should form the habit from his youth up to pray daily for all his needs. We do this not because God needs to be made aware of our needs, but to impress upon us our dependence upon him."

Luther also recognizes prayer as a discipline with a promise. As Luther expresses at the end of the catechism section on the Lord's Prayer, God "himself commanded us to pray like this and promised to hear us." The reformer bases this on the first petition, "Our Father who art in heaven." When asked what does this mean, the answer given is "Here God would encourage us to believe that he is truly our Father and we are truly his children in order that we may approach him boldly and confidently in prayer, even as beloved children approach their dear father." Consequently, we pray because God commanded us to, because we need to, and because we can be confident that our prayers are heard. As he works through each of the phrases of this prayer, he at times adds another question to the familiar, "What does this mean?" as he also asks, "How is this done?" In the process, Luther finds the Lord's Prayer to be a perfect model of prayer, as its various petitions provide an ample reminder of "all the needs that continually beset us, each one so great that it should impel us to keep praying for it all our lives."

After the Lord's Prayer, Luther continues his teaching on Christian practice by addressing the sacraments. Much has been said about the sacraments in earlier chapters. Nestled in between entries on "The Sacrament of Holy Baptism" and "The Sacrament of the Altar" stands a discussion of "Confession and Absolution," which merits discussion here. When we see the same person, known for bringing to light the long obscured doctrine of the priesthood of the believer, saying that we "should say to the confessor, 'Dear Pastor, please hear my confession and declare that my sins are forgiven,'" we may well be perplexed. Consequently, it is worth looking into Luther's thoughts on the matter.

First, we should notice that Luther does not call confession a sacrament. In his treatise *On the Councils and the Church* (1539), he lists confession and absolution, there referred to as the "power of the keys," as one of seven marks of a true church, but even there he does not view it as a sacrament. Secondly, Luther develops his thought here entirely differently from the Roman view. First, he stresses that confession is ultimately to God, and further that God alone grants absolution on Christ's work. Thirdly, Luther follows the instruction given in James 5:16 to "confess our sins one to another."

With these caveats in mind, we can look to his instruction. Luther first informs us that "before God we should acknowledge that we are guilty of all manner of sins, even those of which we are not aware . . . Before the confessor, however, we should confess only those sins of which we have knowledge and which trouble us." To help us become more aware of our sins, Luther compels us to "reflect on [our] condition in light of the Ten Commandments." We may recall that as Luther considers the Ten Commandments, he certainly uncovers much more than a list of ten things to do or not to do. Confession of sin should follow. He adds, however, "If anyone does not feel that his conscience is burdened by such or by greater sins, he should not worry, nor should he search for and invent sins, for this would turn confession into torture." Perhaps nobody knows this condition better than Luther, whose experience at confession as a monk may well be characterized as torture.

Once this confession is made to the pastor, the pastor is to say, "God be merciful to you and strengthen your faith." Then he should ask, "Do you believe that this forgiveness is the forgiveness of God?" Once the person confessing answers, "Yes, I do," the pastor replies, "Be it done for you as you have believed." Again, this may strike us, especially non-Lutherans, as odd, yet it may well be something worth thinking about. In his final comments on confession in the catechism, Luther observes, "A confessor will know additional passages of the Scriptures with which to comfort and strengthen the faith of those whose consciences are heavily burdened or who are distressed and sorely tried." What Luther encourages here is pastoral counseling at its finest, confronting sin with the comfort of Scripture. While we may dismiss the letter of the law concerning Luther on confession, following the spirit of the law on the matter may be of assistance.

In later editions of the catechism, Luther attached sections addressing morning and evening prayers and prayer at the dinner table. Interestingly, Luther advises a prayer of blessing before the meal and a prayer of thanksgiving after the meal. He also added sections on the "Table of Duties." These final points consist "of certain passages of the Scriptures, selected for various estates and conditions of men, by which they may be admonished to do their duties." Drawing upon his conception of the three estates, Luther begins with the priestly estate and the duties of bishops, pastors, and preachers. He follows with instruction on the duties that Christians owe their pastors and teachers. He moves next to the temporal estate, addressing both duties of governing authorities and those of their subjects. He turns to the marital estate, exhorting husbands, wives, parents, and children, as well as laborers, servants, and masters. Finally, he adds sections on youth, widows, and Christians in general. In each table of duties entry, Luther offers not one word of his own advice. He simply collects various Scripture passages, letting the Bible inform us of our duty respecting our various roles in life. *The Small Catechism,* though a short text, comes close to a comprehensive statement on Christian practice.

The Next Generation

Near the end of his life, Luther, in one of his "Table Talk" entries, remarks upon the importance of schools. He observes, "The youth is the church's nursery and fountain-head. When we are dead, where are those who will take our place if there are no schools? Schools are the preservers of the church." He then notes, "Little children have learned at least the Lord's Prayer and the [Apostle's] Creed in the schools and the church has been remarkably preserved through such schools." Through the instruction provided in the catechism, Luther trusts in the future of the church.

In straightforward language, Luther discusses basic texts and basic elements of Christian ethics, doctrine, and practice in order to ensure that the members of future generations know what they believe and the difference those beliefs should make in their lives. In some ways, the rich legacy of Protestantism, thriving and continuing to echo Luther's teachings nearly five centuries later, stands as a testimony to the accomplishment of that goal. His devotion to the task of handing down the teachings of the gospel and orthodox theology to the next generation also stands as a challenge for us as we contemplate not only our present situation, but also our legacy to future generations. While Luther's method of catechetical instruction may not be in vogue today, it remains an effective teaching tool to communicate the essentials of the Christian faith.

Luther made this challenge to the church of his day, a challenge that deserves to be heard in ours:

> We cannot perpetuate [Christian doctrine] unless we train the people who come after us and succeed us in our office and work, so that they in turn may bring up their children successfully. Thus the Word of God and the Christian church will be preserved. Therefore let every head of a household remember that it is his duty, by God's injunction and command, to teach or have taught to his children the things they ought to know.

Luther himself daily devoted time not only to his own children, but also to the children of Wittenberg to rehearse and explain the catechism. In his brief text "Concerning the Order of Public Worship," a text that we will examine shortly, Luther encouraged the parents of Wittenberg to devote Sunday afternoons to catechism instruction. This is a wise practice, which not only serves to teach the young, but also reminds their elders of the same essential truths. In one of the earlier "Table Talk" selections, Luther reports, "Though I am a great doctor, I haven't yet progressed beyond the instruction of children in the Ten Commandments, the Creed, and the Lord's Prayer. I still learn and pray these words everyday with my Hans and my little Lena." Luther also encourages parents to teach their children in a sermon devoted to expositing the elements of the catechism. He intended these sermons "on the fundamentals of Christian knowledge" not to replace the catechetical instruction at home. In fact, he begins the sermons by exhorting parents to take the task of teaching these things to their children seriously. "I admonish you parents," he heralds, that if you "do not help, we shall accomplish little with our preaching, and if I preach all year long and the crowd only comes in and looks at the walls and windows of the church, it is of no use to us."

In the words of *The Small Catechism,* Luther both teaches us the essentials of the Christian faith and models how to teach those truths to the next generation. Luther's own expansive list of professions, including theologian, academic, pastor, musician, and church administrator, should be expanded further to include child educator. Luther, however, would see this last task as simply an extension of his life's work as a preacher of the gospel.

A Note on the Sources

Both *The Large* and *The Small Catechism* may be found in copies of *The Book of Concord,* the confessional standard of Lutheranism. Fortress Press makes both works available as individual texts, entitled *The Small Catechism of Martin Luther* and *The Large Catechism of Martin Luther.* Timothy F. Lull includes *The Small Catechism* in *Martin Luther's Basic Theological Writings* (1989), pages 471–496.

9

DINNER WITH LUTHER

"Table Talk"

"On the first day of August he sat at the table after breakfast, and after some reflection he wrote on the table with chalk: 'Substance and words—Philip [Melanchthon]. Words without substance—Erasmus. Substance without words—Luther.' When he had written this Master Philip and Master Basil happened to come in, and the former said that this is true as far as Erasmus, but too much is attributed to him, and 'words' must also be attributed to Luther."
"Table Talk" recorded by Anthony Lauterbach
and Jerome Weller, August 1, 1537

A S A WEDDING GIFT to his favorite minister and renowned professor, Frederick the Wise turned over the keys to the stately Black Cloister, the former Augustinian monastery at Wittenberg, to Martin Luther. Luther entered this home as a monk in 1508 and, apart from his travels, lived there until his death in 1546. Here he wrote, lectured, prepared sermons, taught children, and, with Katie, reared his family. In the center of the building stands a large clock tower, the same tower where, according to his later recollection, he made the Reformation discovery of justification by faith. One side of the house contained his study, bedrooms, and family rooms. The other featured a very large lecture room and many small ones. Today, it is known as the Luther House, *Lutherhalle,* and stands as a museum to Luther and the Reformation that his discovery in its tower spawned.

Luther's House

Luther entered the Black Cloister as a troubled monk, amidst a corrupt church, struggling to make peace with God. He left it as a married pastor with six children, amidst a new church committed to the gospel, resting in the work of Christ. Katie moved into the Black Cloister on June 13, 1525, her wedding night. It was a huge house and proved a great deal to manage. Seldom, however, was the house empty. The Luthers had six children of their own between the years 1526 to 1534. Four more, orphans of relatives who fell victim to the plague, grew up within its walls. During the plagues that hit Wittenberg, the former monastery, which had been a home and an academy, was transformed yet again into a hospital, with Martin and Katie serving as caregivers, at great personal risk. It was a place for traveling dignitaries, ministers, and friends to lodge, sometimes for extended periods. It also served as a boarding house for numerous students. Luther lectured in the halls on the other side of the tower, and he ruminated over his ideas in his study. And, around its dining room table, some of Luther's best theologizing took place.

In the evenings, everyone in the great house, and friends who dropped by, gathered around the table for the meal. After dinner, Luther and his family usually treated their guests to live music before gathering back around the table for theological discussions lasting well into the night. Katie, on more than one occasion, quipped that her husband should charge tuition for these gatherings. So engaging were these conversations that his students rotated the responsibility of recording them. One visitor described the impression that the host left on those seated at the table: "We used to call his conversation the condiments of the meal because we preferred it to all spices and dainty food."

Out of habit, Luther's students kept notebooks and pens handy as the reformer spoke. At times, Luther even exhorted the scribe to "write this down," as he made various pronouncements. But essentially these writings were private, reflecting the give-and-take of hashing out issues in a casual setting. These records of the conversations were collected and first published after the reformer's death in 1566. Eventually, in the mid-eighteenth century, they were incorporated into the editions containing collected volumes of his writings. Known as the "Table Talk," *Tischreden* in German, these texts are unique like their author and provide unprecedented insight, as well as a vivid picture of Luther's life and thought.

Crumbs from Luther's Table

The first publication of the "Table Talk" appeared as a result of the efforts of John Aurifaber, who served as Luther's personal secretary during the last years of his life. Aurifaber also recorded the events of those last days and Luther's dying words. Various manuscripts, including those of the "Table Talk," also came into his possession. In the preface to the 1566 edition, Aurifaber refers to this rich treasury of conversation manuscripts. He notes that he could "not with good conscience allow this treasure of Luther's table conversation to be hidden." He, consequently, gave it a wider audience in the hopes that "the Christian church, which can be strengthened by such teaching, can use it with blessing as crumbs fallen from Luther's Table, and with it can satisfy the spiritual hunger and thirst of men's souls." Thanks to those student scribes, manuscript compilers, and John Aurifaber, we can eavesdrop on those conversations, and, centuries later, pick up "crumbs from Luther's table."

As a loose collection of conversations, the "Table Talk" by no means reflects a systematic, structured work. The discussion ranges from the family dog to discourses on the christology of the early church fathers. In many entries, Luther reflects on his writings and the key events of his life. These reflections help historians and biographers piece together the development of his thought. While these writings fall short of providing a full scale autobiography, they offer ample material to illuminate crucial times in his life. We want to be careful, however, in trying to use the "Table Talk" to interpret Luther. We must remember that these conversations were recorded by students and published after his death, which means that Luther could not have "approved" them as written. Further, the "Table Talk" has been used to argue that Luther is a manic-depressive, or that he was malaffected by his relationship to his parents. Others see Luther, because of the "Table Talk," as obsessed with his health and physiology, especially his bowels.

This therapeutic approach to understanding Luther owes more to Erik Erikson's book *Young Man Luther,* a highly psychologized portrait based on Erikson's pychoanalysis of Luther in the "Table Talk," than to the actual data. This is not to say that Luther did not suffer bouts of depression, for he did. It is also not to say that he never referred to his bowels, for he did that, too. It is only to say that a psychologized portrayal of Luther based on his "Table Talk" is poor historiography. Rather than putting too much stock in these approaches, we need to remember that only a fraction of

Luther's conversations were recorded, sometimes only a few lines representing a whole evening's worth of conversation. And what was written down, as noted, was not penned by Luther himself. Consequently, a careful approach to interpreting the Luther of the "Table Talk" is in order. The "Table Talk" *should* be read, however, as this material provides an unparalleled glimpse into Luther's life, especially his private life. Here we are introduced to the Luther behind the public persona, an opportunity rarely afforded in the study of historical figures.

As mentioned above, the "Table Talk" entries run the gamut of subjects. A number of entries record interactions with friends and foes alike. Not surprisingly, this material fills in many gaps in the historical record. It also tends to introduce colorful language. In fact, because of some of the language of the "Table Talk," editors expressed reluctance to include the material in collected volumes of Luther's writings. Not wanting to give the papists and his critics any more ammunition, some of his supporters, even centuries after his death, claimed the "Table Talk" to be the clever work of forgers. To be sure, the "Table Talk" does contain vitriolic speech and vulgar language.

Luther himself justifies his language by appealing to his dire circumstances. The Margrave, or prince, Joachim of Brandenburg, one of many dignitaries to join the conversation around Luther's table, once asked the reformer about his strong language. Luther responded with an illustration: "I can cut through a willow branch with a bread knife, but to cut through tough oak requires an axe and a wedge, and even with these one can hardly split it." Urgent situations, argued Luther, call for strong language.

Not all of Luther's colorful language is vulgar. In fact, if you were to extract all the vulgar material in the "Table Talk," it would fill just a few pages of hundreds of pages of text. His humor and wit, however, grace essentially every page. His sarcasm and one-liners well rival the most sophisticated comic, and they undoubtedly made for entertaining and memorable evening discussions. Luther once said, "Tomorrow I have to lecture on the drunkenness of Noah, so I should drink enough this evening to be able to talk about that wickedness as one who knows by experience." His humor, however, usually took the form of stories that he either made up himself or had fun embellishing. For instance, in a discussion with Melanchthon over God's government of the world, he tells the following story:

> Thus the Italians made an arch to please the emperor. On one side was written "Utrecht planted," because it was the birthplace of Adrian. On the other side was inscribed "Louvain watered," because Adrian had studied there. At the top was written, "The emperor gave the growth," because he had made him pope. Then a bad boy came along and scribbled on the bottom of the arch, "Here God did nothing!"

On another occasion he says, "Young fellows are tempted by girls, men who are thirty years old are tempted by gold, when they are forty years old they are tempted by honor and glory, and those who are sixty years old say to themselves, 'What a pious man I have become.' " The one-liners include both humor and proverbial sayings, such as "A lie is like a snowball. The longer it is rolled on the ground the larger it becomes."

A number of the "Table Talk" conversations engage issues related to living the Christian life. Luther addresses prayer, studying Scripture, and the role of suffering, to name just a few. Naturally, controversies and issues regarding church polity and practice surface during those hours around the table, as well. On these topics, Luther dispenses advice much like a doctor writes prescriptions. Finally, the "Table Talk" provides an unparalleled look into Luther's home life. Katie emerges from the pages as one of his most frequent dialogue partners—often to the point of the other guests simply observing a married couple talking theology after dinner. Of course, this was no ordinary couple, and so no ordinary conversation occurred. In fact, these conversations, like so many of his writings, are classic, containing timeless treasures of wisdom. Sometimes, as we have seen, they are stated humorously, other times colorfully, but always in an engaging style. Here is a sampling of some of the rich material found in the "Table Talk."

A Sampling of the Menu

Luther's home life serves as the subject of many entries. He even used the family dog, Tolpel, as a source for instruction. One student secretary records the following: "When Luther's puppy happened to be at the table, he looked for a morsel from his master, and watched his master with open mouth and motionless eyes. Luther then said, 'If I could only pray, the way this dog watches meat! All his thoughts are concentrated on this piece of meat.' " On one occasion, Luther simply dropped out of the conversation altogether to play with his newborn son, Martin. The student secretary records, "Then he played with his infant child and said, 'Oh, this is the best of God's blessings.' " Luther also exclaimed, "I am rich. My God has given me a nun and has added three children." In many of the entries, Luther reflects on his marriage with Katie. He at one point, reflecting on both his marriage and the death of his infant daughter, Elizabeth, expresses both the sweetness and the sorrow that human relationships bring: "There is no sweeter union than that in a good marriage. Nor is there any death more bitter than that which separates a married couple. Only the death of children comes close to this; how much this hurts I have myself experienced."

Not all of the entries concerning his family were of a serious nature. At one point he sarcastically quipped, "If I wanted a more obedient wife, I'd have to hew one from stone." He also offered a number of comments in jest to his colleagues and students. In one entry, he recalls his advice to his publisher's son on his wedding night. He told the bridegroom that he should "be lord in your house." Luther paused, and then added, "Whenever his wife is not at home!" When he was serious, he extolled the virtues of marriage, as evidenced in the following comments: "It's the greatest blessing of God when love continues to flower in marriage." He also praised women, as in the following entry: "Imagine what it would be like without women. The home, cities, economic life, and government would virtually disappear. Men can't do without women. Even if it were possible for men to bear children, they still couldn't do without women."

Other entries present Luther's perspective on numerous theological issues. In particular, Luther's thoughts on the task and nature of theology permeate the "Table Talk." In a discussion of how God may be known, he declares, "[God] is visible in his word and work. Apart from his word and work, one should not look for him." As Luther elsewhere states, "I have the word, and that I let suffice." Christ and his work of redemption serve as the focal point of God's word and work. Luther expresses this well as he observes, "We see that all history presses toward the forgiveness of sins. Everything circles around the center, and that center is Christ." At another point, Luther adds, "Those who don't seek God or the Lord in Christ won't find him." Luther also relates his own journey as a theologian in one entry from the

9.1 Though the presence of the Christmas tree might be questioned, this portrayal of Luther and his family with Philip Melanchthon and others looking on accurately depicts evenings in the Luther home. Engraved by J. Bannister from the original by Schwerdgeburth.

fall months of 1532: "I didn't learn my theology all at once. I had to ponder over it even more deeply, and my spiritual trials [*anfechtungen*] were of help to me in this, for one does not learn anything without practice." He adds, "It is God's greatest gift to have a biblical text and to be able to say, 'This is right. I know it.'"

Luther's Reflections on His Life's Journey

Perhaps the most helpful insight provided in the "Table Talk" concerns Luther's reflections on his own spiritual struggles and his pilgrimage from Rome to the true gospel. During the early months of 1532, one of Luther's students recorded the following:

> Satan often said to me, "What if your teaching by which you've overthrown the pope, the mass, and the monks should be false?" He often assailed me in such a way as to make me break out in sweat. Finally, I answered, "Go and speak with my God, who commanded us to listen to this Christ." Christ must do everything.

Naturally, many of these entries, as in the case here, reference the pope. This antagonism was for him no mere war of words. "You don't understand," Luther tells us near the end of 1542, "what darkness we were under during the papacy." Because of this darkness, Luther entered the fray and challenged the entire papal system. He did this, as he writes, "after careful reflection and in a sufficiently hostile frame of mind."

Of course, this was after the watershed year of 1517 and its aftermath. Before then, Luther was locked in an intense struggle to earn God's grace. The following entry recalls his life as a monk: "I would take a Saturday off, or shut myself in for as long as three days without food and drink, until I had said the prescribed prayers. This made my head split, and as a consequence I could not close my eyes for five nights, lay sick unto death, and went out of my senses." He also recalls vividly his first mass as a priest: "When at length I stood before the altar and was to consecrate, I was so terrified by the words 'to the eternal, living, and true God' that I thought of running away from the altar and said to my prior, 'Reverend Father, I'm afraid, I must leave.' " He then adds, "So terrified was I by those words! Already I had forebodings that something was wrong, but God didn't give me an understanding of this until later."

The "later" eventually came, as God led Luther to understand the doctrine of justification by faith. As Luther said at one point, "What would be easier for a man to say to God than, 'I am a sinful man, but you are a righteous God?'" We don't admit this, however, and instead "we are our own tormenters." He finally learned to stop tormenting himself and to rest in the righteousness of Christ. As he says, "In short, the article of justification by [the work of] Christ solves everything." Reflecting on his posting of the *Ninety-Five Theses* on the Wittenberg church door, Luther exclaims, "God knows, I never thought of going so far as I did. I intended only to attack indulgences. If anybody said to me when I was at the Diet of Worms, 'In a few years you'll have a wife and your own household,' I wouldn't have believed it." But that was precisely the path God had marked out for Martin Luther. The entries of the "Table Talk" provide an extraordinary view into the twists and turns his life took.

Luther and His Disciples

For many reasons, Luther stands out even among other well-known figures of church history. One reason for his prominence, undoubtedly, would be his magnetic personality. The entries of the "Table Talk" reflect his unique and endearing character. Additionally, his table was rarely empty, a further witness to his graciousness and charisma. Not everybody, however, can be Luther. The constant flow of dinner guests would be enough to unnerve most people. But, as we see in the example of those dinner conversations, Luther teaches us that relationships with people matter greatly. And it is here that we see the importance of discipleship for Luther. In the pages of the "Table Talk," Luther models what today goes by the name "mentoring." As the students completed their studies at Wittenberg and returned to their various homes and started in ministry or their professions, they no doubt recalled those evening conversations frequently and were more than likely quite grateful that Luther had invited them into his home.

We should probably add that Luther did not always entertain guests. At times, when Luther felt the pressures of his writing and work, he simply locked himself in his study. One story has it that after a three-day refuge in his study, Katie, frustrated by his absence, took the door off its hinges. But, somehow Luther managed to accomplish much, including spending time with his young and old disciples.

There is one other virtue that Luther teaches us through the "Table Talk." He believed that theology was to be taught and learned. He himself earned his doctorate in theology and was employed primarily as a theologian, spending significant time lecturing on the subject. The "Table Talk" stands as a testimony to his belief that theology should also be lived, and he lived out his theology in full view.

Though it would be much better to be an actual guest at his table, we can at least see and hear Luther from a distance by reading the "Table Talk." As we do, we engage a classic text that well repays our reading.

A Note on the Sources

Not all of the "Table Talk" is translated into English. The standard, and most comprehensive, German edition contains three volumes of material. The standard English edition, *Luther's Works,* only consists of one volume. This volume presents the most thorough collection in English, arranging the entries in chronological fashion. Each set of entries by a student secretary also contains a helpful introduction by the translators and editors.

10

A NEW SONG BEGUN

The Hymns

"A mighty fortress is our God, a bulwark never failing."
Martin Luther, 1527

"After theology, I accord music the
highest place and the greatest honor."
Martin Luther

A RECURRING THEME expressed in this book is that Martin Luther revolutionized not only the theology of the church of his day, but also its practices. Luther's treatment of music in the church is a fine example. In addition to his many other gifts, Luther possessed great musical talent. Some of his friends reported that he was a better musician than a theologian—a comment not so much depreciating his theological ability as much as complimenting his musical skill. In his lifetime he composed thirty-eight hymns, many of which still appear in hymnals today. In addition, he also composed numerous arrangements of medieval antiphons, or verses sung responsively. For many of his hymn texts, Luther also supplied the tune. Among these musical accomplishments stands what may be considered the most beloved hymn of all time, "A Mighty Fortress Is Our God." If only this text survived from all of his writings, we would still perhaps recite his name among the historical figures who have impacted the church.

Singing and making music played an integral role in all of Luther's life. Music filled his home, and for the first time in history it flowed from the grateful hearts of Castle Church parishioners in Wittenberg. It was not unusual for guests at the Luther home to be treated to a concert by the Luther family after dinner. Luther often turned to music as a solace from the currents of conflict swirling about him. And, he especially viewed music as playing a crucial role in the life of the church. The laity listened to the monks or the choirs sing the antiphonies during the mass. Of course, these were sung in Latin, so some may have listened without understanding a word. Because of Luther's reforming work, however, they could not only hear words they could understand, but they could sing them for themselves. This innovation further widened the gulf between Luther and Rome.

Luther would prefer, however, to view congregational singing not as an innovation, but rather a return to and restoration of the biblical practice which was obscured over the centuries. Music was not a mere enhancement to the church service, but played a crucial role in allowing the redeemed to express their gratitude toward God. In an unfinished piece entitled *Concerning Music,* Luther writes, "Music is a gift and largesse of God, not a gift of men. It drives away the devil and makes people happy; it induces one to forget all wrath, unchastity, arrogance, and all other vices. After theology I accord to music the highest place and the greatest honor."

Other elements of the worship service also attracted

Luther's attention. Just as music was kept from the laity, so too prayer was mostly given over to the clergy and the monks. To be sure, the laity prayed. But, prayer as an act of service and of worship was especially the provenance of the professionals, especially the monks who spent their lives in prayer. For the common person, prayer meant little more than reciting the words of the Lord's Prayer in the mass. Luther left a significant mark here, as well. Just as he pointed the way to recover the lost articles of theology that essentially define Christianity, so too he led in restoring the disciplines and practices so crucial to living the Christian life. This chapter explores his contribution as a musician and hymn writer.

Luther, the Musician

The prior and monks at the Augustinian monastery in Antwerp, The Netherlands, supported Luther's teaching and, consequently, after 1521 they fell under the same ban placed on the reformer at the Diet of Worms. While Frederick the Wise looked out for Luther, these monks had no such protector. Imperial troops razed the monastery and imprisoned the monks. They were forced to recant their stand with the heretic Luther or face death at the stake. Most recanted, but three did not. On July 1, 1523, the very first martyrdoms of the Reformation occurred. Once the news reached Luther, he memorialized their testimony of courage and their stand for truth in his first hymn, and the first of the Reformation, "A New Song Shall Here Be Begun." Essentially a ballad, it tells the story of this martyrdom in twelve stanzas. The middle stanzas capture the ballad well:

Their cloister garments off they tore,
Took off their consecrations;
All this the boys were ready for,

They said Amen with patience.
To God their Father they gave thanks,
That they soon would be rescued
From Satan's scoffs and mumming pranks,
With which, in falsehood masked,
The world he so befooleth.
Then gracious God did grant them
To pass true priesthood's border,
And offer up themselves to him,
And enter Christ's own order.

During the next year or so, Luther wrote twenty-three more hymns. While this ballad was Luther's first hymn, his close affinity with music extends back to his early years. He undoubtedly sang in choirs during his early school days. At Erfurt, he received, along with his classmates, instruction in musical theory. His instrument of choice was the lute, an instrument that he mastered and one for which he wrote numerous compositions. He had close relationships with Johann Walther, the first Protestant cantor and "the father of Lutheran church music," and Georg Rhau, a former cantor and publisher at Wittenberg who also is credited as the first music publisher of the Reformation. Walther records that Luther "found great delight in the chorale as well as in figurate music (that is, solo or unison music as well as in part music). I spent many a pleasant hour singing with him and often experienced that he seemingly could not weary of singing or even get enough of it; in addition, he was able to discuss music eloquently."

Luther also greatly admired—and was significantly influenced by—the musical compositions of Josquin de Pres (or Desprez), regarded as the first great composer since the Middle Ages. In a "Table Talk" selection, Luther observes, "God has preached the gospel through music, as may be seen in Josquin, all of whose compositions flow freely, gently, and cheerfully, are not forced or cramped by rules, and are like the song of the finch." Josquin died the same year as the Diet of Worms was conducted, but his work inspired the reformer as he tried his hand at musical composition. An early discovery of the twentieth century reveals a polyphonic composition, among others, attributed to Luther.

Luther even held that one should not be ordained unless he has been trained in music. His view of the importance of music was not shared by his contemporaries, however. Zwingli, though he later repented of the incident, led the charge in the smashing of organs and musical instruments in the cathedrals at Zurich and in Switzerland. Calvin, though he refrained from destroying instruments, nevertheless dismissed them from the church's worship and argued that only the Psalms should be sung in public worship. Luther, too, argued for reform of the medieval approach to music and public worship, but he wanted reform, not dismissal. He wrote, "I am not of the opinion that all arts are to be cast down and destroyed on account of the gospel as some fanatics protest. On the contrary, I would gladly see all arts, especially music, in the service of him who has given and created them." On another occasion, he added, "God has his gospel preached also through the medium of music."

Luther's reforms of music started with what the medieval church bequeathed him, the Roman Mass. He revolutionized this and in 1523 produced "An Order of Mass and Communion for the Church at Wittenberg." In the opening words of this pamphlet, Luther wrote, "It is not now or ever has been our intention to abolish the liturgical service of God completely, but rather to purify the one that is now in use from the wretched accretions which corrupt it." Luther, consequently, offered a recasting of the traditional liturgy in a way that accords with "evangelical use." He retained mostly

Latin for the music, adding only a few German hymns. It soon became apparent to Luther, however, that a completely new liturgy was in order. In 1524, Johann Walther spent nearly a month collaborating with him on the project. On October 29, 1525, the congregation at Wittenberg held its first completely German service. The service's order was published early in 1526 as *The German Mass* and quickly became the standard for the new evangelical churches across German lands. We should not let the word "mass" distract us, though, as we could easily substitute the word "liturgy."

Luther ends the text, complete with suggestions for the order of worship and the sermon, as well as with both lyrics and musical compositions for singing with instruments. His final words offer caution regarding the use of his liturgy. He trusts that it will not become either abused or rote. Instead, he hopes it will "serve for the promotion of faith and love." After the preaching of the Word, he once remarked, sufficient time needs to be given for the congregation to praise God and offer thanks for his work. Singing, he thought, accomplished this best. And he devoted a great deal of time to helping the church offer praise worthy to God. Below follows a treatment of the fruit of his labors as we examine some of his hymns.

Luther's Legacy of Hymns

"A Mighty Fortress" clearly ranks as Luther's most well-known hymn, if not the most well-known hymn of Christianity. It was written in 1527, and some associate it with the months of exile at the Wartburg Castle following the Diet of Worms. Luther's hiding place, the impressive Castle perched high upon the mountain overlooking Eisenach, resonates with the words "a mighty fortress." Additionally, the line informing us that "though this world with devils filled should threaten to undo us, we will not fear, for God has

Fig. 10.1 A Mighty Fortress Is Our God

German Text	English Translation
Ein feste Burg ist unser Gott,	A mighty fortress is our God,
ein guter Wehr und Waffen;	A bulwark never failing;
Er hilft uns frie aus aller Not,	our helper he amid the flood
die uns jetzt hat betroffen.	of mortal ills prevailing.
Der alt bose Feind,	For still our ancient foe,
mit ernst ers jetzt meint;	doth seek to work us woe;
gross Macht und viel List	his craft and power are great;
sein grausam Rustung ist;	and armed with cruel hate,
auf Erd ist nicht seins gleichen	on earth is not his equal.

Putting the English side by side demonstrates the rhyme inherent in the original text. The most well-known English translation by Frederick Henley Hedge, given here, manages to capture a faithful translation of the German, while reflecting the rhyme that exists in the German lines.

willed his truth to triumph through us," clearly evokes both the spiritual battle and the victory during the long months at the Wartburg. The hymn was not written there, however, as it did not appear until five years later. The year in which it was written, 1527, provided Luther with plenty of reasons to look to God as a mighty fortress and a bulwark never failing. The plague that hit the city of Wittenberg, as we saw earlier, had taken its toll. Luther experienced personal illness, and he watched helplessly as his infant son, Hans, battled illness. That year also marked the tenth anniversary of Luther's posting of the *Ninety-Five Theses*. By now he had learned that if he trusted in his own strength, then his "striving would be losing." Instead, he had learned to look to Christ, "the man of God's own choosing."

In many ways, this hymn encapsulates the story of Luther's life. Though he starts with God, the mighty fortress, he quickly moves to express the pain of life, "mortal ills prevailing," and the power of the enemy, "For still our ancient foe doth seek to work us woe." The first stanza even ends on a gloomy note, expressing the reality that there is no match for Satan, as he cries out, "on earth is not his equal." The hymn, however, progresses from this dire realization, stanza by stanza, until it reaches a crescendo of exaltation in ultimate victory. The second stanza finds Luther realizing the key to that victory as he admits his inability and frailty and looks to the one who is able. "Dost ask who that may be?" Luther inquires, "Christ Jesus it is he." He further designates Christ as the Lord of Hosts or Armies, using the designation of Lord Sabaoth. He ends this stanza by expressing his confidence in Christ as "he must win the battle." Yet, before the battle is won, the third stanza reminds us that we are locked in conflict in "this world with devils filled." Even here, however, his hope remains intact, as he ends by heralding that the devil's "rage we can endure, for lo! his doom is sure, one little word shall fell him." The final stanza exalts that word that abides above all earthly powers. In addition, God also grants the Spirit and the gifts to enable us to stand and to deliver us on the final day. So he resolves,

> Let goods and kindred go, this mortal life also;
> The body they may kill; God's truth abideth still;
> His kingdom is forever.

One has to look far and wide to find a hymnal that does not contain "A Mighty Fortress Is Our God." This is not the case with Luther's other thirty-seven hymns. His hymn corpus reflects a variety of topics. He wrote hymns on the Ten Commandments, the Apostle's Creed, and the Lord's Prayer as reinforcements for instructing in the catechism. Other hymns express musically the great doctrines of the faith. Many of the hymns, like the Psalms, praise God for his work. "Dear

10.2 The Wartburg castle served as Luther's "Patmos" during his 1520–22 exile. Perhaps this image served to inspire "A Mighty Fortress" written six years later.

Christians, One and All Rejoice," Luther's second hymn, stands as a good example of this. The first stanza declares:

> Dear Christians, one and all, rejoice, with exultation
> springing,
> And with united heart and voice, and holy rapture singing,
> Proclaim the wonders God hath done, how his right arm
> the victory won,
> Right dearly it hath cost him.

Other hymns also reflect the Psalms recounting David's cries of desperation. Luther's third hymn, "From Trouble Deep, I Cry to Thee," speaks well to this plea. This hymn quickly became associated as a funeral hymn, even serving as one of the hymns for Luther's own funeral service. Within its words, Luther reflects on Psalm 130; the first stanza expresses the sense of desperation:

> From trouble deep I cry to thee, Lord hear thou my crying;
> Thy gracious ear turn to me, open it to my sighing,
> For if thou mean'st to look upon the wrong and evil that
> is done,
> Who, Lord, can stand before thee?

Luther's use of the Psalms foreshadows the strategy of the father of English hymnody, Isaac Watts (1674–1748). Watts utilized the Psalms by "Christianizing" them. His work from 1719, *The Psalms of David Imitated in the New Testament,* explains this as he completed the thought of the Psalms both by making the implicit references to the coming Messiah explicit and by giving clear references to Christ and his work. Luther also, while following the pattern of the Psalms for some of his hymns, explicitly focuses on Christ. In the preface to the first published hymnal of his works, Luther writes, "We may now boast that Christ is our praise and song and say with St. Paul, 1 Corinthians 2:2, that we should know nothing to sing or say, save Jesus Christ, our Savior." This hymn is no exception to this new emphasis. Once Luther expresses his desperation, he confesses his hope, not in his own merit, but on the promise of God's Word:

> Hope therefore in my God I will, on my deserts not
>   founding;
> Upon him shall my heart rely, all on his goodness
>   grounding.
> What his true Word doth promise me, my comfort shall
>   and refuge be.

He offers the fifth and last stanza as a reminder to rest in Christ's work and God's grace:

> Although our sin be great, God's grace is greater to
>   relieve us;
> His hand in helping nothing stays, the hurt however
>   grievous.
> The Shepherd good alone is he, who will at last set Israel
>   free,
> From all their sin and sorrow.

Other hymns reflect Luther's facility as a poet, as well as his abilities as a wordsmith. Along these lines, Luther was quite fond of paradoxes. He often repeated this one attributed to a tenth-century monk: "We say 'In the midst of life, we die.' Whereas, God says, 'No, in the midst of death we live.' " He then turned this seeming contradiction into a hymn, "In the Midst of Life" (1524). He noted that as we live, we "are in death's embrace," an acknowledgment intended to reflect both our physical and spiritual condition. Yet, in the midst of this death, and, as the third stanza adds, even in the "midst of the pains of hell," we can find life. This is because of the ultimate paradox: Christ's death brings about life. Because of Christ's "outpoured and precious blood" we have life in the midst of death:

> In the midst of death behold Hell's jaws gaping at us!
> Who will from such dire distress free and scatheless set us?
> That dost thou, Lord thou only . . .
> In the midst of pains of hell, we our sins are baiting.
> Whither shall we flee away, where a rest is waiting?
> To thee, Lord Christ, to thee only.

These themes of life and death and our victory over death through Christ's work fill the seven stanzas of "Christ Jesus Lay in Death's Strong Bands," from 1524. In the first stanza, Luther explains:

> Christ Jesus lay in death's strong bands, for our offenses given;
> But now at God's right hand he stands and brings us life from heaven;
> Therefore, let us joyful be and sing to God right thankfully,
> Loud songs of hallelujah. Hallelujah!

The second of Luther's seven stanzas, which typically is edited out of modern hymnals, records why Luther declares "Hallelujah!" at the sight of Christ's work:

> No man yet death overcame, all sons of men were helpless;
> Sin for this was all to blame, for no one yet was guiltless;
> So death came that early hour, over us he took up his power;
> And held us all in his kingdom.

The fourth stanza, typically the second in modern hymnals, demonstrates how Christ came to conquer death. Additionally, this stanza continues to play off of the paradox of life and death:

> It was a strange and dreadful strife when life and death
>   contended;
> The victory remained with life, the reign of death was
>   ended;
> Holy Scripture plainly saith, that death was swallowed
>   up by death,
> His sting is lost forever. Hallelujah!

The next few stanzas relate how Christ, the paschal lamb, freely gave his life to set us free from death. Returning to the paradox, in the midst of our lives, there is death. In the midst of Christ's death, there is life, or as Luther put it so eloquently, "His blood on our doorpost lies, faith holds that before death's eyes." Little wonder that Luther ends each of the stanzas of this hymn exclaiming, "Hallelujah!"

Luther's last hymn, penned in 1543, summarizes well his overall desire in writing and singing hymns, offering God praise. This hymn, "Thou Art Three in Unity," is a German version of a traditional hymn for the vespers or evening service, and is a fitting last testament to his hymn writing. The final short stanza heralds:

> To God the Father praise be poured;
> To God the Son, the only Lord;
> To the consoling Holy Ghost;
> Now and forever, ending never.

In between "A New Song Shall Here Be Begun" in 1523 and this hymn from 1543, Luther authored a total of thirty-eight hymns. He also participated in publishing hymnals. He and Johann Walther published the first German hymnal, *Spiritual Hymn Booklet, Geistliche Gesangbuchlein,* in 1524 at Wittenberg. Virtually every year after that another hymnal was produced. These hymnals also included the work of others. It all started with Luther, who, in effect, caused an explosion of creative hymn writing. It was as if his first few hymns and the publication of the first hymnal, with only a handful of hymns, opened the floodgates. In the first hymnal's preface, Luther explains, "I have with the help of others compiled several hymns, so that the holy gospel which by now by the grace of God has arisen anew may be noised and spread abroad." He considered music an extension of the preaching of the gospel. In fact, he knew that it was quite capable of accomplishing much in the service of promoting the gospel. His enemies said, "Luther has done more harm by his songs than by his sermons." "Next to the word of God," he wrote in another hymnal's preface, "music deserves the highest praise."

Singing Luther's Hymns with Understanding

Living five centuries after Luther, we may not realize fully how much we owe him, and others, such as Isaac Watts, the father of English hymnody, who followed Luther's lead. A helpful book that has become a standard on the history of hymnody is Harry Eskew and Hugh McElrath's *Sing with Understanding.* The authors express the book's purpose in the introduction, noting that it serves "to contribute to more meaningful congregational singing of hymns." So this chapter hopes not only to offer some background for the hymns of Luther, but also to engender both an understanding and appreciation of Luther's contribution to the "congregational singing of hymns."

Luther totally redressed the medieval practices of worship and singing in the church. He moved the liturgy off of its faulty theological bases and solidly onto the work of Christ. He wrote hymns and liturgical pieces in the common language so members of the congregation at Wittenberg, as well as throughout Germany, could "sing with understanding." Though we may not fully realize it, as we stand every Lord's day to sing our praise to God, we owe much to Martin Luther. In addition, his hymns, like his other writings, have stood the test of time. Some of them have long since moved out of our hymnals, while others prominently remain. But in all of them, we find words of challenge and comfort, instruction and encouragement. His legacy of hymns extends far beyond a contribution to the worship at the Castle Church in Wittenberg and continues to minister to the church today.

A Note on the Sources

A comprehensive treatment of Luther's hymns may be found in *Luther's Works: Volume 53, Liturgy and Hymns*, Ulrich S. Leupold. Here the reader finds thorough discussions of Luther's works on the Latin and German mass, as well as brief introductions and the complete lyrics in English translation of all of Luther's thirty-eight hymns. The hymnals with the most hymns by Luther are, of course, those serving various Lutheran churches. Marilyn K. Stulken's *Hymnal Companion to the Lutheran Book of Worship* (1981) offers both technical and historical discussions of Luther's contributions to hymnody. Two helpful books on hymnody in general are Donald Hustad's *Jubilate!* (1981), and Eskew and McElrath's *Sing with Understanding* (1980).

11

THE MARKS OF A
TRUE CHURCH

On the Councils and the Church

"We can spare everything except the Word."
Martin Luther, 1523

O N OCTOBER 5, 1544, the New Castle Church in
Torgau held its dedicatory service. Leonard Koppe,
the fish merchant who, along with Luther, made
it possible for twelve nuns to escape from the convent at
Grimma, lived there. Since 1517 it also had been a center
of Luther's supporters and a stronghold of his ideas. Now
it was the first city to construct an Evangelical or Lutheran
Church. Naturally, only one person would be best suited
to preach the message for its dedication. After just a few
words of greeting, Martin Luther declared, "The purpose of
this New House may be such that nothing else may happen
in it except that our Lord himself may speak to us through
his Holy Word and we respond to him through prayer and

praise." For Luther, this comprised the mission and purpose of the church.

The Missing Ingredient

Every time the church gathers, Luther wrote, God's Word needs to be preached, or Christians should not even come together. Clearly in response to the medieval church, which had misplaced the Word of God, Luther placed the Word at the very heart of the church's practice and life. The Word of God was, for him, the true mark of the church. In fact, in 1527 he declared, "The only perpetual and infallible mark of the church was always the Word." As he developed his doctrine of the church, he also expanded his view of the marks of the church. As early as 1520, he moved from solely emphasizing the Word alone as *the* mark to including the two sacraments of baptism and the Lord's Supper. By 1539, in *On the Councils and the Church,* he expanded the list to include four more marks. Then in 1541, he further enlarged the list to include no fewer than ten marks that distinguish the true church. If it were not for his death in 1546, perhaps his list would have grown even longer.

This discussion concerning the marks of the true church was, for Luther, a crucial one. In a sense, his entire quarrel with Rome may be summed up by the one question it raises: What does the true church look like? In his view, Rome had veered so far off the mark that no vestige of the true church remained. Consequently, he could not reform it from within. He had to make a clean break and construct a new church altogether. While the heart of the church was dead, Luther found much in the practice of the church worth salvaging, which he in turn instituted in his church. Yet, even these practices were not borrowed without serious overhaul. The discussion of Luther on the Lord's Supper addressed earlier bears this out. As well, his understanding of confession, just viewed in the previous chapter on *The Small Catechism*, expresses how he transformed old practices to be more reflective of biblical teaching. Given his insistence on the priesthood of all believers, the fact that he condones confession of sin to a priest perhaps surprises and confounds us. Looking at his understanding of confession, however, shows that Luther and Rome were worlds apart.

This example illustrates how Luther adopted the practices of the medieval church while simultaneously reconstructing them so as to be more reflective of the biblical picture of the church. Beyond these sorely abused practices, however, the Roman church lost the key ingredient, the preaching of the Word, which obscured if not altogether shut out the doctrine of justification by faith. Once the center of the church was restored, however, much work remained concerning the rest of the structure. Luther's legacy to the church includes material aimed at reconstructing not only the center, but also the periphery. His writings on the church, not unexpectedly, literally fill volumes. For our purposes we will explore mainly two works, "Concerning the Order of Public Worship" (1523) and *On the Councils and the Church* (1539), to hear Luther's instruction on what the church should both look like and do.

Meeting at 5:00 A.M.

The church service provides a helpful place to start. Luther introduced many innovations regarding the church service. Congregational singing, preaching and singing in the common language rather than solely in Latin, and the preaching of the Word—all of which we take for granted—were virtually unheard of until Luther brought them into the church. Some had attempted instituting these reforms. For instance, John Hus made congregational singing a regular part of the church's practice at Bethlehem Chapel in Prague. For this, however, he was condemned as a heretic and the practice did not last. Also, as Luther would acknowledge, his new practices were not really innovations, but rather a return to biblical models. We should also mention that while Luther advocated the use of the common language in the church service, he did not forbid the use of Latin altogether. In fact, he even desired for part of the service to include Greek and Hebrew.

Although Luther wanted a multilingual service, he could not accomplish this. He also desired the church to meet at 4:00 a.m. He could not pull that off, either; he managed, however, to convince the congregation at Wittenberg to meet at 5:00 a.m. Apparently, rising early was one of the few practices of monastery life that Luther wanted to retain. He did not just prescribe this early morning service for Sunday alone, however, as he wanted it to become a daily exercise. On Sunday he scheduled two services, the first at 5:00 a.m. and the second, the "late service," at 9:00 a.m. Luther admonished the families of Wittenberg to devote Sunday afternoons to the catechism. These ideas derive from his brief text from 1523, "Concerning the Order of Public Worship." The church service that he outlines in this text goes back, he argues, to "genuine Christian beginnings." By Luther's day, however, the church service became corrupt. He identifies three specific abuses, including first the silence of the Word of God, next the introduction of non-Christian legends and fables in the place of God's Word, and finally the view of the mass as a work by which one might merit God's grace and win salvation. "In order to correct these abuses," he proposes "that a Christian congregation should never gather together without the preaching of God's Word and prayer." Luther further proposes that the preaching of God's Word includes the entire

Bible. In fact, he suggests that the various books of the Bible be presented until "the entire Bible has been read through." All of this will produce the following result: "Christians will by daily training become proficient, skillful, and well versed in the Bible. For this is how genuine Christians were made in former times and could also be made today."

As Luther's directions for the service unfolds, he carefully avoids setting up a dogmatic schedule. Nevertheless, he suggests that the service begin with preaching, or the reading and interpreting of the Bible. He adds that this should last about half an hour. Luther does not advocate long-winded sermons. In a "Table Talk" conversation regarding preaching, he quips, "When I have nothing more to say I stop talking." After this Luther recommends, "The Congregation shall unite in giving thanks to God, in praising him, and in praying for the fruits of the Word." This involves singing the Psalms, hymns, and antiphons—liturgical songs sung in a response format. The whole service, Luther notes, should be "completed in one hour or whatever time seems desirable; for we must not overload souls or weary them. As was the case in monasteries and convents where they burdened themselves like mules."

The congregation should meet not only in the early morning, but also in the evening. Luther suggests that the order of worship for the morning be followed in the evening, as well. Again, as he prescribes boundaries, he refrains from establishing rigid rules for an order of worship. Instead, he offers a flexible approach, "as long as the Word of God be given free reign to uplift and quicken souls so that they do not become weary." In addition to the morning and evening services, Luther also suggests the option of a service after the lunch hour. If people are going to church three times daily, we might well ask if that leaves any time to get things done. We need to remember, however, that the medieval model

Fig. 11.1 Marks of the True Church

"The only perpetual and infallible mark of the church was always the Word." –Martin Luther, 1527.

1520	1539	1541
On the Papacy in Rome	*On the Councils and the Church*	*Against Hanswurst*
1 The Word of God	1 The Word of God	1 Office of preaching and God's Word
2 Baptism	2 Baptism	2 Baptism
3 The Lord's Supper	3 The Lord's Supper	3 The Lord's Supper
	4 The Power of the Keys	4 The Power of the Keys
	5 Calling and Ordination of Pastors	
	6 Prayer, Praise, and Thanks to God	
	7 Enduring the Cross and Spiritual Struggle	
		5 Apostle's Creed
		6 Lord's Prayer
		7 Honor to Temporal Authorities
		8 Praise of Marriage
		9 Suffering of the True Church
		10 Not Seeking Revenge from Persecution

included the daily mass and evening vespers. Further, we need to add that Luther fully expected that not everyone could attend all of these services. Finally, the reformer believed that people should only attend "willingly and not reluctantly, or by constraint, or for the sake of reward, temporal or eternal, but alone to the glory of God and the neighbor's good."

Luther hoped, however, that the entire congregation would gather together on Sunday. He further advised that he preferred the Lord's Supper be administered on Sunday only, replacing the daily mass with the preaching of the Word. As he observes, "Let everything be done so that the Word may have the free course instead of the prattling and rattling that has been the rule up to now." He ends his brief discussion with a colorful application of the Mary and Martha story from Luke 10. From this story he concludes that "one thing is needful," and that is to "sit at the feet of Christ and hear his word daily. This is the best part to choose and it shall not be taken away forever. It is an eternal Word. Everything else must pass away, no matter how much care and trouble it may give Martha."

As we reflect on Luther's advice concerning the church service, we may not decide to follow it, especially the 5:00 a.m. meeting time. His consistent and thorough emphasis on the centrality of the Word, however, well repays following. Many things can distract the church of any age; the church in our age is no exception. As Luther warns, "We can spare everything except the word." Not only is the Word central to the church service, it stands as the crucial mark of the true church. This discussion of the true church occupies much of Luther's writings. In the following pages, we'll explore his thoughts on this issue.

The Marks of the True Church

By 1539, a few decades had passed since Luther launched his first salvo against the church. He remained resolved that Rome's problem boiled down to the question of authority. For Rome, authority derived from the church as the interpreter and guardian of Scripture. The councils and the popes, in other words, tradition, offered guidance for the church. For Luther, authority resided in Scripture alone (*sola Scriptura*). This was his position while debating John Eck in Leipzig in 1519 and at the Diet of Worms in 1521, and it remained his position throughout his life. We see this point clearly in his treatise *On the Councils and the Church,* 1539. A large work in three parts, this volume reveals the problems inherent in simply returning to the church fathers to reform the church. It also features Luther's dabbling in church history as he discusses the early ecumenical councils and sets forth the marks of the true church.

In the first part, Luther tackles the humanist's challenge not to start a new church altogether, but simply to return to the church of the early church fathers. Luther expresses the humanist's sentiment this way: "There are (in my opinion) several good, pious souls who would like to see the church reformed on the pattern of these same councils and fathers, as they too are aware that the present position of the church in the papacy is woefully at variance (as is evident) with the ways of the councils and the fathers." He concludes, however, that such an approach will not suffice. Firstly, Luther pointed out that the fathers, as well as the councils, disagree and do not speak with one voice on many issues. Secondly, and more importantly, he notes that the fathers themselves pointed beyond their own work to Scripture. Now his intent is not to ignore the valuable teaching that can be gained from studying the church fathers and councils; he simply argues that the church needs to move beyond them to the Scriptures themselves for a true reformation.

Luther's appreciation of church history becomes clear in the second part of the treatise as he surveys the great councils of the church, starting with the Council at Jerusalem as recorded in Acts 15 and ending with the Council at Chalcedon in 451, and including Nicea (325), Constantinople (381), and Ephesus (431) in between. His interest in church history was

Courtesy of the Pitts Theology Library, Candler School of Theology

11.2 This portrait of a Lutheran worship service well captures Luther's lasting legacy

both for his personal enrichment and for his self-preservation. In his early debates with Cajetan and Eck, as well in his various pamphlet wars, Luther was consistently accused of being out of step with church tradition. This drove him to study the tradition, and he found, although his Roman opponents did not always admit it, that in many respects it was he who was in step and they who were not. Luther used his knowledge of church history in this present work to show that the councils protected the church from the christological heresies. They relied not upon their own authority, however, but upon that of Scripture.

Luther then turns his attention to the church in the third part of the treatise. He begins by asking what the word *church* means. He answers, playing off the Greek word's meaning, that it is an assembly, or a called-out people. He then notes that Christians "are a people with a special call and are therefore called not just *ecclesia*, 'church,' or 'people,' but *sancta catholica Christiana,* that is, 'a Christian holy people' who believe in Christ." Here, Luther appeals to both the words of the Apostle's Creed, "I believe . . . in the holy catholic church," and Augustine's teaching on the four marks of the true church as one, holy, universal or catholic, and apostolic church. Augustine's view, however, begs the question. One is still left evaluating what constitutes the one, holy, universal, and apostolic church. Luther, perhaps recognizing this shortcoming in Augustine's discussion of marks of the true church, offers a sevenfold litmus test to determine whether a given church is, in fact, God's holy people.

The first mark, as we might imagine, concerns the preaching of the Word. Luther even goes further, exclaiming, "Now wherever you see or hear this word preached, believed, professed, and lived, do not doubt that the true 'Christian holy people' must be there." This "chief holy possession" of the church, Luther observes, "purges, sustains, nourishes, strengthens, and protects the church." The second and third marks are the sacraments of baptism and the Lord's Supper respectively.

Luther's fourth mark may cause one to pause as he expresses, "Fourth, God's people or holy Christians are recognized by the office of the keys exercised publicly." This perhaps sounds Catholic to us. We need to understand, however, what Luther intends by it. First, he does not mean the power of the keys as understood by the Roman church as the power of the Pope. "The keys belong not to the pope (as he lies)," observes Luther, "but to the church, that is, God's people." Luther then defines the keys as involving confession and absolution of sin, noting, "As Christ decrees in Matthew 18, if a Christian sins, he should be reproved; and if he does not mend his ways, he should be bound in his sin and cast out. If he does mend his ways, he should be absolved. That is the office of the keys."

Fifthly, "The church is recognized externally by the fact that it consecrates or calls ministers, or has offices that it is to administer." Luther devotes much time here to criticizing the Roman view of the clergy, including the issue of celibacy. He concludes that Rome has clouded the biblical teaching. He also here counters certain Anabaptist or fanatical strains that would eliminate the clergy altogether in reaction against Rome. As Luther states, "The church cannot be without these bishops, pastors, preachers, priests; and conversely, they cannot be without the church." The sixth mark concerns "prayer, public praise, and thanksgiving to God." He then explains the various ways this mark manifests itself:

> Where you see and hear the Lord's Prayer prayed and taught; or Psalms or other spiritual songs sung, in accordance with the word of God and the true faith; also the [Apostle's] Creed, the Ten Commandments, and the catechism used in public, you may rest assured that a holy Christian people of God are present.

The seventh and last mark of the true church involves what Luther refers to "as the holy possession of the sacred cross." By this he means recognizing that suffering is part of the Christian's life. As he writes, members of the true church "must endure every misfortune and persecution, all kinds of trials and evil from the devil, the world, and the flesh." This suffering "mortifies the old Adam and teaches him patience, humility, gentleness, praise and thanks." It further enables us "to learn to believe in God, to trust him, to love him, and to place our hope in him." Further, suffering stands in stark contrast to the papacy and the excesses of Rome.

These seven marks are more than a litmus test; they also serve as the goal of the church. As Luther challenges us, "We constantly strive to attain the goal, under his redemption or remission of sin, until we too shall one day be perfectly holy and no longer stand in need of forgiveness." Luther gives Christians who desire to be a gathering of holy people, a church, much to consider. These seven marks represent well the teaching that Christians are not only a holy people, but also a peculiar people—a people who may well go against the grain, who stand out for their commitment to principles not derived from their environment, but from the Word of God.

Luther adds several more marks of the true church in a curiously titled treatise from 1541, *Against Hanswurst*. The German word *Hanswurst* means a carnival figure or clown. This word was first used derogatorily in reference to Luther's relationship to John Frederick, the Elector of Saxony. Duke Henry of Braunschweig/Wolfenbuttel, committed to the Catholic position and closely associated with Emperor Charles V, had opposed the Reformation and Luther from the beginning. He continually contended against the other German rulers in favor of the Catholic lands. In 1540, he wrote a criticism of John Frederick in which he vainly tried to pit John Frederick against Luther by falsely accusing Luther of referring to John Frederick as his *Hanswurst,* his clown, or his fool. At first Luther was reluctant to respond, saying, "I do not think that this vile fellow is worth a syllable's reply." Luther, however, eventually saw value in answering Duke Henry. He wrote a lengthy criticism of him, turning the tables, and referring to Duke Henry as the real *Hanswurst.*

Luther spends a considerable part of this work relentlessly attacking Duke Henry and pointing out his errors.

But then he uses the platform this exposure provided him to once again launch into one of his key themes: the marks of the true church as portrayed in the Bible versus the present activity in the Church of Rome. Luther admits that the Catholic church of his day came from the ancient, true church. He also admits that it has many of the same practices that he labels as marks of the true church, such as baptism, the Lord's Supper, and the creed. He then intones, in his own inimitable way, "But you are no longer of the church, or members of the church, for in this holy church of God you are building your own new apostate church, the devil's brothel with limitless whoredom, idolatry, and innovation." Luther here uses irony to refer to the practices of the Catholic church, though centuries old, as new. His designation of the Catholic church as a whoredom, a not so veiled reference to Revelation 17, spills over this treatise's pages.

Luther also uses this treatise to promote what the true church should look like. In the process, he adds three more marks: honor to temporal authorities, praise of marriage, and not seeking revenge for persecution. The first mark is most likely due to the context of the *Hanswurst* comment by Duke Henry. The second mark also may be included because of the context, as Duke Henry reportedly took a mistress, a report that later turned out to be true. The final mark derives from the broader historical situation, as Luther's followers continued to experience persecution. He still, however, persists in emphasizing the preaching of the Word as the penultimate mark of the true church. "The church," Luther again reminds us, "must teach God's Word alone." He then points to the character traits that such teaching produces, namely humility and reverence. He concludes, "The true sign of the holy church has always been humility and fear in the Word of God."

Through his discussion of the marks of the true church, Luther entered an historical conversation stretching back to Augustine and continuing to the present day. In the Reformation context, Luther's insistence on the centrality of the Word was followed by John Knox in Scotland and John Calvin in Geneva. Calvin, like Luther, added the sacraments for a total of two marks. Knox also added the sacraments, but additionally viewed church discipline as a mark, creating a list of three marks of the true church. Later the Puritans in New England followed suit with Luther's emphasis on the centrality of the preaching of the Word. They constructed their churches in a way that people entering would immediately have their attention drawn to the pulpit. This was designed explicitly to underscore the centrality of preaching.

Returning to the reformer and his context: Luther warned that Rome's problem was not that it lacked the true marks, but that the practice of those marks had been perverted through adding human traditions. Consequently, he continually reminded his own generation to keep Scripture central. He further stressed this so that generations to come would not fall prey to the same temptation to displace the preaching of the Word. Following Luther's advice, as we look to Scripture, we see the same words in Paul's admonition to his young disciple, Timothy, from 2 Timothy 4:2, "Preach the Word." This advice is as true today as it was in Luther's generation.

A Note on the Sources

Luther's writings aimed exclusively at the nature of the church and its practice are collected in *Luther's Works: Volumes 39–41, Church and Ministry I–III*. *On the Papacy in Rome* may be found in Volume 39, 49–104; *On the Councils and the Church* in Volume 41, 3–178; and *Against Hanswurst* in Volume 41, 179–256. A helpful introduction by Eric W. Gritsch accompanies each of these texts. Timothy F. Lull includes a number of selections related to Luther's thought on the church, including Part III of *On the Councils and the Church* in *Martin Luther's Basic Theological Writings* (1989), pages 414–575.

12

THE RELUCTANT PASTOR

The Sermons

"The world will see us preachers as fools and unworthy, that opens the door for God to be seen as just, wise, and merciful."
Martin Luther

W E REALIZE LUTHER was a prolific sermon writer when we consider these statistics. Just over 200 sermon manuscripts survive from Luther's hand for the years 1510–1522. From the years 1522 to 1546, scholars estimate that Luther preached an additional 5,800 sermons. Of these 6,000 or so sermons, full manuscripts, stenographer's notes, and rough texts, about 2,000 remain. The Weimar Edition of Luther's works, the authoritative and most complete German Edition, devotes sixteen volumes exclusively to sermons, and also places sermon material elsewhere in the edition. In one of the "Table Talk" entries, Luther *explains* how he produced so many sermons: "Often I preached four sermons on one day. During the whole of Lent, I preached two sermons and gave one lecture each day." He has been called by many one of the best preachers of all time. Though some may debate this designation, few would doubt that he remains among the most prolific preachers in history.

Luther delivered many sermons in the Castle Church at Wittenberg. Additionally, he preached many more in his home, the former Black Cloister. When he traveled, he was always asked to preach. In his last trip, to Eisleben, he preached four times in just a few days—despite the illness that claimed his life days later. He first started preaching regularly in the Black Cloister when he was named sub-prior at the monastery in 1512. He may have preached prior to this time during his years at the Erfurt monastery. Most scholars date his first sermon to 1510, however. Just after Luther began preaching in the Black Cloister, Frederick the Wise encouraged the City Council of Wittenberg to designate him as the parish pastor for the Castle Church. Luther held that post officially until 1522, when he gladly gave the title and main responsibilities to his friend, Johannes Bugenhagen. In practice, however, Luther continued to preach numerous times, typically three to five times weekly.

Luther reluctantly became a pastor. Reflecting on his call to preach, he referred to Moses's call. Luther mentions Moses's reluctance, but not in a way to criticize him. In fact, Luther interjects, "Had I been in Moses's shoes, I would have hired a lawyer to file a complaint against God." He adds elsewhere, "God had to ask Moses as many as six times. He also led me into the office in the same way." As Luther looks back on his time spent as a minister, however, he confesses, "When I regard him who called me, I would not take the whole world not to have begun as a minister." As a pastor, he understood his task as staying very focused. He once defined a minister as "one who is placed in the church for the preaching of the Word and the administration of the sacrament." And to him, preaching the Word meant preaching

Christ. We will be taking a closer look at Luther's thoughts on the ministry and on the task of preaching shortly. Also, from the 2,000 or so sermon manuscripts, we will look at just one representative sermon to get a sense of what the residents of Wittenberg enjoyed regularly.

Luther on Preachers and Preaching

Luther and his listeners did not always enjoy a harmonious relationship. In one sermon from 1530, Luther expressed his frustration at their indifference toward his exhortations. In his typical parlance, he told them that to keep preaching to them in their seeming indifference "annoys me." His frustration grew so great that year that he refused to preach at the Castle Church for quite some time. In one of the "Table Talk" selections he observes that most sermon listeners are Epicureans: they like preaching that helps them live easily, whereas challenging preaching is not always welcome. These disillusioning experiences led Luther to write, "If I were to write about the burdens of the preacher as I have experienced them and as I know them, I would scare everybody off." It was not, however, a completely rocky road. When Luther went on his "strike" from preaching, he soon heard clamoring for his return and he once again ascended the pulpit.

Luther reflected often on the nature of preaching and preachers. He thought that sermons should be understandable and bearable, aimed at the audience. He often warned against long-winded preaching: "Don't torment your hearers, or keep them sitting in church with long, tedious sermons. Such preaching robs the pulpit of delight." In his brief text "Concerning the Order of Public Worship," as we saw earlier, Luther suggested that the service be kept to an hour and the preaching to half that time so as "to not overload souls or weary them." He also instructed his students to "preach

12.1 Woodcuts appeared frequently throughout the early editions of Luther's German Bible. This one, probably by Lucas Cranach, illustrated Genesis 22 for the 1523 printing of the German Old Testament. This image of Abraham slaying Isaac and the text are used frequently in Luther's sermons.

about things that are suited to a given place and given persons." He recalls that he once heard a "preacher who gave an exhortation in praise of marriage to some aged women in an infirmary." Luther also advocated colorful preaching. He often made the biblical characters and stories come to life for the congregation at Wittenberg and in the *Lutherhalle*.

Historian Roland Bainton calls attention to one such memorable sermon concerning the nativity and the text, "There was no room for them in the inn." Luther baited his audience by offering a stinging chastisement of the innkeepers, as well as Bethlehem generally, for not making room for Christ. His listeners were undoubtedly shaking their heads in agreement. Luther continued, "There are many of you who think to yourselves: 'If only I had been there! How quick I would have been to help the Baby! I would have washed his linen.'" He then challenged, "Yes, you would. You say that because you know how great Christ is, but if you had been there at that time you would have done no better than the people of Bethlehem." He then made an application: "You have Christ in your neighbor. You ought to serve him, for what you do to your neighbor in need, you do to Christ himself."

Similarly, Luther retold the Genesis 22 story and the command to Abraham to sacrifice Isaac. He noted, "Abraham was told by God that he must sacrifice the son of his old age by a miracle, the seed through whom he was to become the father of kings and of a great nation. Abraham turned pale. Not only would he lose his son, but God appeared to be a liar." Luther continued telling the story, vividly relaying the details. Then he reached the climax of the event:

> The father raised the knife. The boy bared his throat. If God had slept an instant, the lad would have been dead. I could not have watched. I am not able in my thoughts to follow. The lad was as a sheep for the slaughter. Never in

history was there such obedience, save only in Christ. But God was watching, and all the angels. The father raised his knife; the boy did not wince. The angel cried, "Abraham, Abraham!" See how divine majesty is at hand in the hour of death. We say, "In the midst of life we die." God answers, "Nay, in the midst of death, we live."

On another occasion he used an illustration to which most of his listeners could relate. He explained:

> Now notice how the natural clucking hen acts; hardly any other creature is so anxious about her young. She changes her natural voice and takes a pitiable and complaining voice; she seeks, scratches, and calls her little chickens; when she finds anything, she does not eat it herself, she leaves it for her little ones; with all earnestness she battles and cries against the buzzard, and spreads her wings out so willingly and lets her chicks crawl under and upon her, and gladly suffers them to stay there. This is a lovely picture.

Luther then made the application of this intense provision and protection to Christ's activity toward believers:

> So it is also with Christ. He has changed his voice to a pitiable tone, has sighed for us and preached repentance, pointed out to everyone their sins and misery, he scratches in the Scriptures and calls us unto them and permits us to eat; he spreads his wings with all his righteousness, merit and grace over us, and takes us lovingly under his protection.

Imagine the impact of such preaching. He was once asked by a student at his dinner table what the secret to good preaching was. Luther answered, "The first commandment:

'I am the Lord your God.' God is firm and unbending towards the wicked; God is kind and merciful towards the righteous. This explains why we preach hellfire to the proud and haughty, paradise to the godly, reproof to the wicked, comfort to the righteous." He continued with an apt illustration: "We have different tools in our workbenches. Some knives cut better than others." Luther had a knack for knowing which tool to use when. In addition to revealing the secret of good preaching, Luther also outlined a method for preaching effectively. He writes,

> First bring the concern into clear focus. Second, define the concern visually, and then make it walk, so men see it in action. Third, show that the concern is scriptural, which gives it authority. Fourth, give examples to explain and thus burn it onto minds. Fifth, make it aesthetic with tropes and metaphors. Sixth, warn the unaware, wake up the sleepy, and shake up the disobedient.

Above all, Luther taught that preaching was to exalt the Word. "A good preacher," he once observed, "invests everything in the Word." As we recall from an earlier chapter, Luther advocated flexibility when it came to the church service on every point except one: "We can spare everything except the Word." Preaching the Word, for Luther, meant preaching Christ. In fact, Christ should not only mark one's preaching, but one's life. As he once remarked, "For a good preacher must be committed to this, that nothing is dearer to him than Christ and the life to come." As one reads through Luther's sermons, you see the overwhelming emphasis on Christ, his work, and our response. One of Luther's most frequently issued sermons, "A Sermon on How to Contemplate Christ's Holy Sufferings," captures this theme of his preaching, and to it we now turn.

Contemplating Christ's Sufferings

Luther preached this sermon in 1519 while the storms of controversy raged about him. This date also virtually parallels Luther's discovery of justification by faith. This sermon proved extremely popular in his day. In fact, no fewer than nineteen separate pamphlet editions date from the year Luther preached it. It continued to enjoy a wide audience and a rich publishing history, making it one of Luther's most frequently published sermons. Luther first preached it on Good Friday, and as the published editions circulated throughout Germany, it undoubtedly was preached by many other ministers on the same annual occasion. The sermon contains seventeen points by Luther. While this sounds cumbersome, each of the points consists of but one paragraph. These seventeen paragraphs can be arranged in two main parts: the first ones concern how not to contemplate Christ's sufferings as Luther presents "false views." The second ones then turn to the "true views," or the proper way to think about Christ's sufferings.

In less capable hands, a sermon on Christ's death on the cross could easily be turned into a sensationalistic treatment aimed at emotional appeal. Certainly, Luther portrays the horrors of the cross, yet as the sermon unfolds, he evokes a response from the congregation that resonates long after the sermon ends. He engages the whole person, expounding the implications of Christ's suffering not just as a past event, but as the foundation for the entire Christian life. By the sermon's end, Luther wants us to contemplate Christ's sufferings not just as we listen to it or read it centuries later, but also as we go about our day, our week, our entire lives.

Luther presents three false ways to view Christ's suffering. He begins, "In the first place, some reflect upon the sufferings of Christ in a way that they become angry with the Jews, sing and lament about poor Judas, and are then satisfied." Luther, unfortunately, did not always heed his own warning not to view Christ's death this way. As we saw earlier, his treatment of the Jews was at times less than desirable. Here in 1519, however, he states that such an approach to Christ's sufferings misses the point completely. The second false view concerns the apparent practice by some simply to meditate on Christ's sufferings in the expectation that suffering in one's own life can be avoided. Luther explains that this approach views Christ's sufferings as a talisman which causes people to "imagine that they thus protect themselves from perils of water, of fire, and of the sword, and all other dangers. In this way the suffering of Christ is to work in them an absence of suffering." These same people falsely believe "that to think once on the sufferings of Christ is better than to fast a whole year or to pray the Psalter everyday." In other words, contemplating Christ's suffering at the Easter season satisfies one's spiritual duty for the year.

Luther addresses the purely sentimental approach to Christ and his work at the cross in the third false view. In Luther's words, "A third class so sympathizes with Christ as to weep and lament for him because he was so innocent." Luther proceeds to rebuke this group for abusing the mass, thinking that "it is enough if they attend mass." And Luther responds, "What help is it to you, that God is God, if he is not God to you?" His point is clearly that this approach fails to see "the true fruit" in Christ's passion. The level of emotion this group experiences never rises above pity for Christ. Consequently, it fails to contemplate the true meaning of Christ's suffering. Luther only devotes a few pages to addressing how not to consider Christ's work. He devotes a great deal more space to how to view it properly.

Terror and Comfort

Luther, in keeping with his penchant for paradoxes, teaches that contemplating Christ's sufferings properly leaves us both terror-stricken and comforted. The terror arises when we acknowledge and confront our sin; comfort comes when we rest in Christ and see our sin atoned for by him. He develops this point as he considers the proper way to contemplate Christ's suffering.

When he turns to the proper response, he does not shrink from portraying Christ's agony. This is Good Friday, not Easter Sunday. So he begins this section by declaring, "They meditate on the passion of Christ aright, who so view Christ that they become terror-stricken in heart at the sight, and their conscience sinks in despair." Luther, however, intends this terror to be turned toward us, in realization that our sin caused God to pour out his wrath on his Son. He continues, "This terror-stricken feeling should spring forth, so that you see the severe wrath and the unchangeable earnestness of God in regard to sin and sinners, in that he was unwilling that his only and dearly beloved Son should set sinners free unless he paid the costly ransom for them." He adds that as one reflects upon how "God's Son, the eternal wisdom of the father, himself suffers, you will indeed be terror-stricken; and the more you reflect the deeper will be the impression."

Luther makes this general understanding of sin specific and personal as he exhorts a Christian to "deeply believe and never doubt the least that you are the one who thus martyred Christ. For your sins most surely did it." Luther appeals here to the example of Peter in Acts 2:36–37, who "struck and terrified the Jews as with a thunderbolt" as he proclaimed that they were the ones who crucified Christ. Luther wants his hearers to see further that God's wrath poured out on Christ will also be poured out on sinners "who let Christ's suffering be lost and fruitless." He vividly portrays such suffering: "Where one thorn pierces Christ, there more than a thousand thorns should pierce you, indeed, eternally and even more painfully."

Throughout this section of the sermon, Luther focuses on the terror to impress upon us our sin, which, he believes, we have grown numb to, even unaware of. He offers the following illustration:

> If an evildoer were judged because he had slain the child of a prince or a king, and you were in safety, and sang and played, as if you were entirely innocent, until one seized you in a horrible manner and convinced you that you had enabled the wicked person to do the act, behold then, you would be in the greatest straits.

Luther identifies us as the one singing and playing, anesthetized to our guilt. In addition to the illustration, he also appeals to one of the few medieval theologians he quoted approvingly, Bernard of Clairvaux. Luther remarks,

> Bernard was so terror-stricken by Christ's sufferings that he said, "I imagined I was secure and I knew nothing of the eternal judgment passed upon me in heaven, until I saw the eternal Son of God took mercy upon me, stepped forward and offered himself on my behalf in the same judgment. Ah, it does not become me still to play or feel secure."

Luther quotes a hymn often attributed to Bernard. The hymn that Bernard is most well known for, "O Sacred Head, Now Wounded," expresses the same ideas as Luther's sermon. The first lines of the second stanza capture the thought well: "What thou, my Lord, has suffered was all for sinners' gain; mine, mine was the transgression, but thine the deadly pain." Luther takes great measures to spell out our need to be terror-stricken in order that we may "come to a true knowledge" of ourselves. Until "we seek that knowledge, the sufferings of Christ have become of no true benefit." Luther has strong words for one who is "so hard-hearted that he is not terror-stricken by Christ's sufferings." He writes that such a person should "fear and tremble," because at some point, either now or at death, there needs to be a reckoning. Luther's pastoral concerns outstrip any desire to downplay or whitewash either Christ's sufferings or the penalty of sin.

Before he leaves this section treating the response of terror and moves on to comfort, he strikes a hopeful chord. First, he says that viewing Christ's suffering properly "accomplishes its true, natural and noble work, it slays the old Adam, banishes all lust, pleasure, and security that one may obtain from other creatures." He also notes that it forces us to look beyond our own abilities and "seek and long for the grace of God." By the time Luther arrives at the twelfth paragraph, this chord of hope becomes a full symphony, as he leads us from Good Friday to Easter Sunday; he does not leave us wallowing in sin, but brings us to Christ. He heralds the good news: "Just as the knowledge of our sins flowed out of Christ and we became conscious of them, so should we pour them again upon him and set our consciences free."

Firm in Christ

Luther explained the unhealthy consequence of failing to do this, when he noted, "For if you do not take this course, but miss the opportunity of stilling your heart, then you will never secure peace, and yet must finally despair in doubt." "But," he observes, "when we see that our sins are laid on Christ and he has triumphed over them by his resurrection and we fearlessly believe it, then they are dead and become as nothing." And as we look to the resurrected Christ, we see "no sin in him, that is no sign of sin." As Paul teaches in Colossians 2:14, Christ has nailed our sin to the cross, and canceled it out. This new perspective on Christ's work brings about a new perspective on God, as his goodness and love take center stage. This, in turn, produces a new motive for service: love. Luther expressed it this way: "So will your heart be filled with love toward him, and the assurance of your faith strengthened." He adds, "When your heart has become firm in Christ, then you are an enemy of sin out of love, and not out of fear of punishment."

As Luther concludes his sermon, he explains that in order to view Christ's sufferings truly, we need to live in light of the cross: "Christ's sufferings should also be an example for your whole life." He not only tells his hearers to do this, but he also shows them how by making direct application from Christ's sufferings to their lives. He does this in a series of probing questions:

Does pride attack you? Behold how your Lord was disgraced and mocked by murderers. Do unchastity and lust, the sins of the flesh, attack you? Think how bitter it was for Christ to have his tender flesh torn, pierced, and beaten again and again. Do hatred and envy war against you, or do you seek revenge? Remember how Christ with many tears and cries prayed for his enemies. If sadness or physical or spiritual hardships distress you, then strengthen your heart and say, "Why then should I not then suffer a little, since my Lord sweat blood in the Garden of Gethsemane because of anxiety and grief?"

This realization, Luther tells us, is how "one can find strength and comfort in Christ against every vice and weakness. This is the right observance of Christ's passion, and the fruit of his suffering." "Christ's passion," he concludes, "must not be dealt with in words and a show, but in our lives and in truth." While Luther, in this sermon, resonates with deep emotions, he also moves far beyond just eliciting an emotional response. Rather, he confronts us with our sin and its ugly consequences. He also comforts us with the salve of the gospel, exalting the goodness and love of God. Finally, he challenges us to live in light of the cross, moving beyond an Easter meditation to a lifetime of gratitude and obedience.

Choosing only one sermon from the thousands that Luther preached poses a serious challenge. Hopefully, this one sufficiently whets the appetite to explore more. Luther's legacy, as we have seen, endures. He excelled as a theologian, translator, musician, and, among other things, as a pastor. His sheer volume of sermons impresses upon us the value he ascribed to preaching. His recovery of the centrality of Scripture for the church also brought with it the recovery of the centrality of the sermon. Just as he pioneered so many of our church practices, so it is with his preaching. It stands as yet another legacy that enriches our lives as Protestants, centuries after Luther, the reluctant pastor.

A Note on the Sources

As mentioned earlier, Luther's sermons form a significant body of literature. In *Luther's Works*, Volumes 51 and 52 are designated for the sermons, but sermons appear throughout many of the other volumes, as well. *The Complete Sermons of Martin Luther*, by Baker Books (2000), includes a previously published edition of Luther's sermons, including *The Sermons of Martin Luther* (1983), and also *The Sermons of Martin Luther: The House Postils* (1996). This set comprises the most exhaustive collection of Luther's sermons in English. Volume 1.2 contains "A Sermon on How to Contemplate Christ's Holy Sufferings," 183–92. John Dillenberger offers a good sampling of Luther's sermons in *Martin Luther: Selections from His Writings* (1962), 207–48. Timothy F. Lull compiles a number of sermons in his reader, including the sermon on contemplating Christ's sufferings, which he titles "A Meditation on Christ's Passion," in *Martin Luther's Basic Theological Writings* (1989), 165–72.

PART FOUR

LUTHER'S *NINETY-FIVE THESES*

T RADITION HAS IT THAT one evening Martin Luther, while walking the streets of Wittenberg, happened on a parishioner lying drunk in the gutter. As Luther rebuked him for public drunkenness, his parishioner fumbled around in his coat. Finally his hand emerged holding a piece of paper. He waved it before his priest, proclaiming that Brother Tetzel had issued him an indulgence that offered "complete forgiveness of all sins—past, present and future." Such a scene, as depicted in the 1955 classic, black-and-white film *Martin Luther*, may be difficult to verify. It illustrates, however, the dilemma facing the young parish priest and theologian. In response, Luther retreated to his study, wrote a list of arguments to address this problem, and the next day, October 31, 1517, nailed his list to the church door at Wittenberg. That was five hundred years ago.

While Luther intended the *Ninety-Five Theses* to spark an academic debate among theologians, his interests and motivations were intensely pastoral. The indulgence sale obscured the gospel and the cross. It led the laity astray. In his "Sermon on Indulgences" given in 1518, Luther references the early attacks to his *Ninety-Five Theses*. He says such "blathering is no big deal." Then he adds, in characteristic fashion, "The ones doing this are some darkened minds, who have never even smelled a Bible." The *Ninety-Five Theses* lays the groundwork for the Reformation's emphasis on *sola Scriptura*, which in turn leads to *solus Christus*—shorthand for the gospel. This is what the church needs.

Little did Luther realize the outcome of his action. By confronting the medieval Roman Catholic Church, he was challenging one of the largest political and ecclesiastical machines the world has ever seen. His action on that last day in October set the stage for a century of upheaval in Germany and across Europe. In fact, repercussions of Luther's actions still ring out today. All who call themselves Protestants trace their roots to this protest in the *Ninety-Five Theses*.

Martin Luther intended that these arguments, written in Latin, be directed toward church scholars for debate. He prefaced his arguments with a request that "those who cannot be present to debate orally with us will do so by letter." That debate never materialized. The arguments, entitled *Disputation on the Power and Efficacy of Indulgences* and known popularly as the *Ninety-Five Theses*, were translated into German, printed (the printing press had been developed relatively recently), and rapidly circulated throughout the cities and villages of Germany. This was only the beginning: by posting the *Ninety-Five Theses*, the young Augustinian monk set in motion one of the most significant events of western history, the Protestant Reformation.

The *Ninety-Five Theses* is a text that everyone knows of, most refer to, but few actually read. Such a crucial text, though, deserves to be read widely. Today's readers might be surprised that the arguments lack the crystallized expression

FIG. 48.— WITTENBERG. (From an old engraving.)

13.1 Wittenberg on the Elbe River (1546). Reproduced from Julius Theodor Köstlin, *Life of Luther* (New York: Scribner's, 1913), where it is said to be "from an old engraving."

of the later Reformation doctrines, such as justification by faith alone. Also, Luther assumes his readers are aware of medieval theology, as well as events of the first two decades of the sixteenth century. Consequently, this edition offers explanatory notes to help readers navigate the text. To set the *Ninety-Five Theses* in its historical context, we begin with a brief look at the life of Martin Luther and the events in and around 1517.

13

THE ANNOTATED
NINETY-FIVE THESES

Disputation on the Power and
Efficacy of Indulgences

Lthough Martin Luther wrote the original *Ninety-Five Theses* in Latin, German translations and numerous reprints followed. Further translations, including texts in English, have been coming off the press since the sixteenth century. Today the document is one of the most prominent texts in western church history. The text that follows is loosely based on the English translation of Adolph Spaeth, L. D. Reed, and Henry Eyster Jacobs. At places I offer my own renderings of their text, providing a readable English version while striving to preserve the intent of the original.

While Luther posted the theses to prompt a debate, the preface underscores his pastoral concerns. His underlying concern was for the truth to prevail over error.

1 The quote from Matthew 4:17 comes from the Vulgate, the authoritative Latin translation. The Latin reads, *Penitentiam agite*, which may be translated, "Do penance." Thus this translation lends credence to the medieval Roman Catholic sacrament of penance. In his *Explanations of the Ninety-Five Theses* (1518), Luther notes that the Greek text means simply "repent," as translated in most English versions of the Bible. Luther is arguing that penance, or merely outward acts, is not in accord with scriptural teaching concerning the forgiveness of sin. True repentance, or that which God requires, is a heart change followed by a life of obedience. The next three theses address the question of repentance. Luther makes his point clear: buying indulgences is in no way equivalent to inward repentance.

2 In 1439 at the Council of Florence, the Roman Catholic Church sanctioned seven sacraments: (1) baptism, (2) confirmation, (3) priesthood or ordination, (4) the eucharist or the Lord's Supper, (5) marriage, (6) extreme unction or last rites, and (7) penance or confession. Luther, along with the other Reformers, reduces this list to the two biblically sanctioned sacraments of (1) the Lord's Supper and (2) baptism. Luther's point in this thesis and those that follow is that the current practice of indulgences is an abuse of the doctrine of penance.

Out of love for the truth and the desire to bring it to light, the following propositions will be discussed at Wittenberg, under the oversight of the Reverend Father Martin Luther, Master of Arts and of Sacred Theology, & Lecturer on these subjects at Wittenberg.

Wherefore he requests that those who are unable to be present and debate orally with us, may do so by letter.

In the Name of Our Lord Jesus Christ. Amen.

1. When our Lord and Master Jesus Christ said "Repent," he intended that the entire life of believers should be repentance.

2. This word repentance cannot be understood to mean the sacrament of penance, or the act of confession and satisfaction administered by the priests.

3 Luther sees the connection between the inward change of heart and the external life of obedience, which he characterizes here in the language of Romans 6–7 as putting the flesh to death. Throughout his writings Luther addresses this same issue, but uses the terminology of law and gospel. Typically he is interpreted as emphasizing gospel and deprecating law, especially after salvation. His emphasis on the life of obedience here, however, needs to be considered in the discussion.

4 Luther makes a rather complex point that risks misunderstanding. In his *Explanations* he clarifies his meaning of hating the self: "True sorrow must spring from the goodness and mercies of God, especially from the wounds of Christ, so that man comes first of all to a sense of his own ingratitude in view of divine goodness and thereupon to hatred of himself and love of the kindness of God. Then tears will flow and he will hate himself from the very depths of his heart, yet without despair. Then he will hate sin, not because of the punishment but because of his regard for the goodness of God; and when he has perceived this he will be preserved from despair and will despise himself most ardently, yet joyfully."

5 Luther speaks directly to the pope's authority to pardon sin and remit punishment in purgatory. In the process Luther shows that Tetzel's indulgences are invalid. The word *canons* refers to Canon Law, the body of laws governing the Roman Catholic Church. By Luther's time the canons would encompass various decretals made by the popes and councils. In 1520 Luther publicly burned the *Corpus iurus canonici*, or the Book of Canon Law, along with the papal bull condemning him as a heretic.

3. Yet it does not mean inward repentance only, as there is no inward repentance that does not manifest itself outwardly through various mortifications of the flesh.

4. The penalty of sin, therefore, continues so long as hatred of self, or true inward repentance, continues, and it continues until our entrance into the kingdom of heaven.

5. The pope does not intend to remit, and cannot remit, any penalties except those that he has imposed either by his own authority or by the authority of the canons.

6 Medieval Roman Catholic theology distinguished between the concepts of guilt and penalty for sin. Guilt could only be remitted or forgiven by God, whereas the penalty for sin is paid for in either this life or purgatory. Theoretically indulgences were only to satisfy the penalty for sin. Indulgence preachers, however, gave the impression that they also satisfied the guilt for sin.

7 At this time Luther advocates the mediation of a priest. As his theology develops, he moves toward advocating the priesthood of all believers.

8 Luther addresses in theses 8–13 the abusive practices of the sacrament of penance and its corollary, indulgences. The penitential canons, or the church's dogma of penance, restrict penance and forgiveness to eternal punishment. This change in the church's practice is referenced in thesis 11.

10 Luther calls the indulgence sale "wicked." In his letter to Albert, Archbishop of Mainz, dated October 31, 1517, he writes, "In this way, Excellent Father, souls committed to your care are being directed to death."

12 Luther's point draws attention to the fact that forgiveness or absolution theoretically follows contrition and satisfaction. Tetzel's indulgence offers forgiveness without any true sorrow for sin or works of satisfaction.

6. The pope cannot remit any guilt, except by declaring that it has been remitted by God and by assenting to God's work of remission. To be sure, however, the pope may grant remission in cases reserved to his judgment. If his right to grant remission in such cases was disregarded, the guilt would remain entirely unforgiven.

7. God remits guilt to no one whom he does not at the same time humble in all things and also bring him into subjection to his vicar, the priest.

8. The penitential canons are imposed only on the living, and according to them nothing should be imposed on the dying.

9. Therefore the Holy Spirit through the pope is kind to us, because in his decrees he always makes exception of the article of death and of necessity.

10. Ignorant and wicked are the acts of those priests who, in the case of the dying, reserve canonical penances for purgatory.

11. This changing of the canonical penalty to the penalty of purgatory is quite evidently one of the tares that were sown while the bishops slept.

12. In former times the canonical penalties were imposed not after but before absolution, as tests of true contrition.

13. The dying are freed by death from all penalties. They are already dead to canonical laws and have a right to be released from them.

14 Luther discusses the abuse of penance by focusing on purgatory in theses 14–24. Tetzel's indulgence claimed that it provided "total remission of all sins for souls in purgatory." Luther concludes in thesis 24 that there simply is no basis for this claim.

16 Luther articulates a significant distinction between purgatory and heaven. They are not on a continuum. Heaven is security, while purgatory is despair.

20 Luther repeats his argument in thesis 5. Church law allows only for forgiveness of church-imposed penalties but not for forgiveness of penalties before God.

21 Though he does not explicitly name Tetzel in the *Ninety-Five Theses*, Luther clearly has him in view when he refers to preachers, or at one point to "hawkers" (thesis 51), of indulgences.

14. The imperfect spiritual health, or the imperfect love, of the dying person necessarily brings with it great fear; and the smaller the love, the greater is the fear.

15. This fear and horror is sufficient in itself alone, to say nothing of other things, to constitute the penalty of purgatory, since it is very near to the horror of despair.

16. Hell, purgatory, and heaven seem to differ as do despair, near despair, and the assurance of safety.

17. Concerning souls in purgatory, it seems necessary that horror should grow less and love increase.

18. It seems unproved, either by reason or Scripture, that they are outside the state of merit, that is, of increasing love.

19. Again, it seems unproved that souls in purgatory, or at least that all of them, are certain or assured of their own blessedness, though we may be quite certain of it.

20. Therefore by "full remission of all penalties" the pope means not actually "of all," but only of those penalties imposed by himself.

21. Therefore those preachers of indulgences are in error, who say that by the pope's indulgences a man is freed from every penalty and is saved.

22. In fact, the pope remits no penalty for the souls in purgatory that, according to the canons, they would have had to pay in this life.

24 Luther's reference to the "high-sounding promise" underscores the invalid claims of the indulgence sale. This is an example par excellence of false advertising.

26 The phrase "the power of the keys" refers to the Roman Catholic interpretation of Matthew 16:16–19. By Luther's day this phrase meant the exclusive power given to the church to forgive sin and dispense the blessings and benefits of the gospel. Luther is not denying that the power of the keys primarily resides in the pope. Instead, he is arguing that the pope's exercise of this power does not extend to purgatory.

27 Luther refers to Tetzel's marketing jingle. The phrase was rather catchy in German:

> *Solbald das Geld in Kasten klingt,*
> *Die Seel' aus dem Fegfeuer springt.*
> As soon as the money in the chest rings (clinks),
> A soul from purgatory springs.

29 Luther refers to the legend of two earlier popes, Severinus (638–640) and Paschal I (817–824), which holds that they were willing to endure a longer time of suffering in purgatory in order to enjoy a greater degree of glory in heaven.

31 Luther's use of sarcasm stresses the worthlessness of the indulgence sale.

23. If it is at all possible to grant to anyone the remission of all penalties whatsoever, it is certain that this remission can be granted only to the most perfect, that is, to the very few.

24. Therefore, the greater part of the people are necessarily deceived by that indiscriminate and high-sounding promise of release from penalty.

25. The power that the pope has in a general way over purgatory is just like the power that any bishop or curate has in a particular way over his own diocese or parish.

26. The pope does well when he grants remission to souls in purgatory, not by the power of the keys, which in this case he does not possess, but by way of intercession.

27. They preach man-made doctrines who say that so soon as the coin jingles into the money-box, the soul flies out of purgatory.

28. It is certain that when the coin jingles into the money-box, greed and avarice can be increased, but the result of the intercession of the church is in the power of God alone.

29. Who knows whether all the souls in purgatory wish to be bought out of it, as in the legend of Sts. Severinus and Paschal?

30. No one is sure that his own contrition is sincere, much less that he can attain full remission.

31. As the man who is truly repentant is rare, so rare also is the man who truly buys indulgences. Indeed, such men are most rare.

32 Luther uses *pardon* interchangeably with *indulgence*.

33 Luther is literally warning, "Buyer, beware."

35 No contrition is necessary on behalf of the one who simply throws coins into the indulgence chest.

37 "All the benefits of Christ . . ." The Reformers will come to emphasize the doctrine of union with Christ. The root of that rich expression is here in this phrase and in thesis 37. Luther first learned this phrase (participatio omnium bonorum Christi) from Thomas Aquinas.

39 This point summarizes the dilemma facing Luther as a parish priest. He had to accept the indulgence letters granted by Tetzel to his own parishioners, yet at the same time he was responsible, as their priest, to remind them of their need of true penance.

32. They will be condemned eternally, together with their teachers, who believe themselves sure of their salvation because they have letters of pardon.

33. Men must be on their guard against those who say that the pope's pardons are that inestimable gift of God by which man is reconciled to him;

34. For these graces of pardon concern only the penalties of sacramental satisfaction, and these are appointed by man.

35. They preach no Christian doctrine who teach that contrition is not necessary in those who intend to buy souls out of purgatory or to buy confessional privileges.

36. Every truly repentant Christian has a right to full remission of penalty and guilt, even without letters of pardon.

37. Every true Christian, whether living or dead, has part in all the benefits of Christ and the church; and this is granted to him by God, even without letters of pardon.

38. Nevertheless, the remission and participation in the benefits of the church, which are granted by the pope, are in no way to be despised, for they are, as I have said, the declaration of divine remission.

39. It is very difficult, even for the most educated theologians, at one and the same time to commend to the people the abundance of pardons and also the need of true contrition.

42 Luther moves beyond merely presenting arguments for debate in theses 42–51 as he offers his own summary of what Christians should be taught. As a monk he extols the virtues of caring for the poor and needy. He also points out that such virtues conflict with the conspicuous wealth of the papacy.

43 Luther continues his rhythm with the recurring phrase Christians are to be taught. Here we again see Luther's pastoral concerns.

45 With poetic irony, Luther references the parable of the Good Samaritan (Luke 10:25–37).

47 Luther expands on this thought in his "Sermon on Indulgences and Grace" from 1518. There he notes that according to church law indulgences are "permitted and allowed," rather than "commanded."

40. True contrition seeks and loves penalties, but liberal pardons only relax penalties and cause them to be hated, or at least they give a reason for hating them.

41. Papal indulgences are to be preached with caution, so that the people may not falsely think of them as preferable to other good works of love.

42. Christians are to be taught that the pope does not intend the buying of pardons to be compared in any way to works of mercy.

43. Christians are to be taught that he who gives to the poor or lends to the needy does a better work than buying pardons;

44. Because love grows by works of love, man becomes better by doing works of love. By buying pardons, however, man does not grow better, only more free from penalty.

45. Christians are to be taught that he who sees a man in need and passes him by and gives his money for pardons instead, purchases not the indulgences of the pope, but the indignation of God.

46. Christians are to be taught that unless they have more money than they need, they are bound to reserve what is necessary for their own families, and by no means to squander it on pardons.

47. Christians are to be taught that the buying of pardons is a matter of free will, not of commandment.

50 This marks the first of several explicit references to the cost of building St. Peter's Basilica. Although it is not entirely clear to what extent Luther was aware of the dealings of Leo X and Albert of Mainz that led to Tetzel's indulgence sale, he and others were well aware of the ulterior motive underlying it.

51 "Cajole money" refers to the underhanded and manipulative techniques of Tetzel and the indulgence preachers.

53 Though far from advocating the Reformation principle of *sola Scriptura* (Scripture alone), Luther emphasizes the necessity and centrality of the Word.

48. Christians are to be taught that the pope, in granting pardons, needs and therefore desires their devout prayer for him more than their money.

49. Christians are to be taught that the pope's pardons are useful so long as they do not put their trust in them; but altogether harmful if they lose their fear of God because of them.

50. Christians are to be taught that if the pope knew the exactions of the indulgence preachers, he would rather that St. Peter's church should go to ashes than that it should be built up with the skin, flesh, and bones of his sheep.

51. Christians are to be taught that it would be the pope's wish, as it is his duty, to give of his own money to many of those from whom certain hawkers of pardons cajole money, even though the church of St. Peter might have to be sold.

52. The assurance of salvation by letters of pardon is vain, even though the indulgence commissary or the pope himself were to stake his soul upon it.

53. They are enemies of Christ and the pope who bid the Word of God to be silent in some churches in order that pardons may be preached in others.

54. Injury is done to the Word of God when, in the same sermon, an equal or a longer time is spent on pardons than on the Word.

55 The mention of the bell, processions, and ceremonies, as well as the reference to the cross emblazoned with the papal arms in thesis 79, refers to Tetzel's entrance into a city. His arrival was first preceded by the announcement of his coming. He was then escorted to the center of town in a parade flanked by the town's political and ecclesiastical dignitaries. The ceremony was so elaborate that one eyewitness in the town of St. Anneberg records that "God himself could not have been welcomed with greater honor."

56 The phrase "treasures of the church" refers to the medieval Roman Catholic teaching that the surplus merits of Christ and the saints are kept in a heavenly treasury. This explains why Roman Catholics pray to and appeal to saints, especially Mary. In Luther's day the pope could withdraw from this treasury and apply these excess and unused merits to those who fell short and needed more. The withdrawal of merits usually came by way of financial contributions to the church. Luther rejects this whole view outright when he argues in thesis 62 that the true treasure of the church is the gospel.

59 St. Laurence was martyred in 258. According to legend (now widely rejected), when ordered by Roman officials to turn over the church's riches, he gathered the church's poor.

62 In his letter to Albert, also written on October 31, 1517, Luther declares, "For Christ nowhere commanded indulgences to be preached, but he strongly commanded the gospel to be preached."

63 Matthew 20:16 ("So the last shall be first, and the first last"—ASV).

55. It must be the pope's intention that if pardons, which are a very small thing, are celebrated with one bell, single processions, and ceremonies, then the gospel, which is the very greatest thing, should be preached with a hundred bells, a hundred processions, and a hundred ceremonies.

56. The treasures of the church, out of which the pope grants indulgences, are not sufficiently named or known among the people of Christ.

57. That they are not temporal treasures is certainly evident, for many vendors do not pour out such treasures so easily, but only gather them.

58. Nor are they the merits of Christ and the saints, for even without the pope, these always work grace for the inner man, and the cross, death, and hell for the outward man.

59. St. Laurence said that the treasures of the church were the church's poor, but he spoke according to the usage of the word in his own time.

60. Without being rash we say that the keys of the church, given by Christ's merit, are that treasure;

61. For it is clear that the power of the pope is in itself sufficient for the remission of penalties and of cases reserved for his jurisdiction.

62. The true treasure of the church is the most holy gospel of the glory and grace of God.

63. But this treasure is naturally most odious, for it makes the first to be last.

66 Luther uncovers the motive of the indulgence sale: to get profits.

69 This reflects the pastoral concern. Priests are bound to recognize these pardons, yet these pardons are illegitimate and harmful and, Luther would say, damning.

71 In theses 71–74 Luther affirms indulgences when practiced legitimately, while condemning Tetzel's illegitimate practice of indulgences.

73 The indulgence sale was accompanied by the document "The Summary Instruction," prepared by Albert and his theologians for the indulgence sale preachers. Luther managed to secure a copy. In the "Summary," the indulgence preachers are promised the Pope's protection.

64. On the other hand, the treasure of indulgences is naturally most acceptable, for it makes the last to be first.

65. Therefore the treasures of the gospel are nets with which they would formerly fish for men of riches.

66. The treasures of the indulgences are nets with which they now fish for the riches of men.

67. The indulgences that the preachers cry as the "greatest graces" are known to be truly such, insofar as they promote gain.

68. In truth, however, they are the absolute smallest graces compared with the grace of God and the piety of the cross.

69. Bishops and curates are bound to admit the commissaries of papal pardons with all reverence.

70. But still more are they bound to strain all their eyes and attend with all their ears, lest these men preach their own dreams instead of the pope's commission.

71. Let him who speaks against the truth of papal pardons be anathema and accursed!

72. But let him who guards against the lust and license of the pardon-preachers be blessed!

73. The pope justly thunders against those who, by any means, contrive harm to the traffic of pardons.

75 With these examples, Luther carries the implications of the indulgence sale to their absurd end.

76 Roman Catholic theology distinguishes between venial sins, which can be forgiven, and mortal or deadly sins, which cannot be forgiven.

78 The reference is to the gift of the gospel, the gift of offices in the church, and the gift of gifts in the church (1 Corinthians 12:28).

79 Luther has used the word *blasphemy* multiple times—and for good cause. The indulgence sale is a false gospel obscuring the cross and the true gospel.

80 See James 3:1.

81 Luther here introduces a series of "shrewd questions" posed by the laity, which he rehearses in theses 82–89. Evidently the common person was well aware of the scandal of Tetzel's indulgences. Further, these points again reveal the financial motives underlying the indulgence sale as Luther makes explicit reference to the cost of building St. Peter's—a cost, according to thesis 86, borne in part by the poor peasants of Germany.

74. But much more does he intend to thunder against those who use the pretext of pardons to contrive injury to holy love and truth.

75. To consider the papal pardons so great that they could absolve a man even if he had committed an impossible sin and violated the Mother of God is madness.

76. We say, on the contrary, that the papal pardons are not able to remove the very least of venial sins, so far as its guilt is concerned.

77. It is said that even St. Peter, if he were now pope, could not bestow greater graces. This is blasphemy against St. Peter and against the pope.

78. We say, on the contrary, that even the present pope, and any pope at all, has greater graces at his disposal: namely, the gospel, powers, gifts of healing, etc., as it is written in 1 Corinthians 12.

79. To say that the cross emblazoned with the papal arms, which is set up by the preachers of indulgences, is of equal worth with the cross of Christ, is blasphemy.

80. Bishops, curates, and theologians who allow such talk to be spread among the people will have to account for this.

81. This unbridled preaching of pardons makes it difficult, even for learned men, to rescue the reverence due to the pope from slander, or even from the shrewd questions of the laity.

83 Church law prohibited praying for the souls of saints (part of the redeemed).

84 Concern for souls in purgatory is not the motivation of the indulgence preachers. The motive is money.

85 The extent of the illegitimacy of the indulgence sale seems to be boundless. This sale, for instance, forgives church penalties long since abrogated.

86 Leo X was a member of the wealthy and prominent Medici family.

87 Luther's use of "participation" refers back to thesis 37. The church must preach contrition, not sell indulgences.

82. Such questions as the following: "Why does the pope not empty purgatory, for the sake of holy love and for the sake of desperate souls that are there, if he redeems an infinite number of souls for the sake of miserable money with which to build a church? The former reasons would be most just, while the latter is most trivial."

83. Or: "Why are funeral and anniversary masses for the dead continued, and why does he not return or permit the withdrawal of the endowments founded on their behalf, since it is wrong to pray for the redeemed?"

84. Or: "What is this new piety of God and the pope, that for money they allow a man who is impious and their enemy to buy out of purgatory the pious soul of a friend of God, and do not rather, because of that pious and beloved soul's own need, free it for pure love's sake?"

85. Or: "Why are the penitential canons, long since in actual fact and through disuse abrogated and dead, now satisfied by the granting of indulgences, as though they were still alive and in force?"

86. Or: "Why does not the pope, whose wealth today is greater than the riches of the richest, build this one basilica of St. Peter with his own money, rather than with the money of poor believers?"

87. Or: "What does the pope remit, and what participation in the benefits of the church does he grant, to those who, by perfect contrition, have a right to full remission and participation?"

90 Luther's call for "reasonable answers" testifies to his desire for a debate. Luther attempts to inform the church of the damage being caused by the indulgence sale.

92 Jeremiah 6:14 ("They have healed also the hurt of my people slightly, saying, Peace, peace; when there is no peace"—ASV).

93 Luther's rather poetic ending hints at what would become the very center of his theology: the cross. In this early stage Luther contends that indulgences promise glory without suffering, while he understands Scripture to teach that glory comes only after suffering. Luther ends where he began with the first thesis: challenging the Roman Catholic understanding of repentance and forgiveness, and offering a radical alternative. For more on Luther's theology of the cross, see his *Heidelberg Disputation* (1518).

94 In his "Sermon on Indulgences and Grace" (1518), Luther declares, "Let the lazy and sleepy Christians buy indulgences. You run from them."

95 Luther's closing statement underscores that he does not wholly understand justification by faith. By his own admission it would be another two years before his personal theological breakthrough and his recovery of this essential doctrine.

88. Or: "What greater blessing could come to the church than if the pope were to do a hundred times a day what he now does once, and bestow on every believer these remissions and participation?"

89. Or finally: "Since the pope, by his pardons, seeks the salvation of souls rather than money, why does he suspend the indulgences and pardons granted prior to now, since these have equal efficacy?"

90. To repress these convincing arguments of the laity by force alone, and not to resolve them by giving reasonable answers, is to expose the church and the pope to the ridicule of their enemies, and to leave Christians unsatisfied.

91. If, therefore, pardons were preached according to the spirit and mind of the pope, all these doubts would be readily resolved. Indeed, they would not exist.

92. Away, then, with all those prophets who say to the people of Christ, "Peace, peace," and there is no peace!

93. Blessed be all those prophets who say to the people of Christ, "Cross, cross," and there is no cross!

94. Christians are to be exhorted to be diligent in following Christ, their Head, through penalties, death, and hell;

95. And thus be confident of entering into heaven through many tribulations, rather than through the false assurance of peace.

A BRIEF GUIDE TO BOOKS BY
AND ABOUT MARTIN LUTHER

*"A student who doesn't want his work to go for nothing ought
to read and reread some good author until the author becomes
part, as it were, of his flesh and blood. Scattered reading confuses
more than it teaches. Many books, even good ones, have the
same effect on the student. So he is like the man who dwells
everywhere and therefore dwells nowhere. Just as in human
society we don't enjoy the fellowship of every friend every day,
but only of a few chosen ones, so we ought to do in our studies."*
Martin Luther, "Table Talk," 1533

T HE WRITINGS OF MARTIN LUTHER literally fill many
bookshelves. Consequently, certain of his writings
simply could not be addressed here. Many others
have been mentioned in the previous chapters, but only too
briefly. The selection has been purposeful, as an exhaustive account would unduly burden both reader and writer.
Commenting on Luther's themes, someone once said he was
a one-note theologian. Of course, various interpreters hold

different perspectives on that one note. It is true, however, that as we read Luther's writings, certain themes, such as the theology of the cross, justification by faith, the centrality of Scripture, and the sacraments, meet us at virtually every turn. Nevertheless, referring to him as a one-note theologian overstates the matter and does not show a proper appreciation for the rich variety of his writings. This book simply serves as an introduction to those writings, and in these last few pages some further guidance is offered to assist those who like what they have read and want to explore more. We begin with Luther's own writings and then turn to those written about him.

Books by Luther

Everything we read by Luther in English is a translation of either Latin or German. Collected Latin editions of his works first appeared in his own lifetime, as did collected German editions. The most ambitious of these projects is the *Weimar Ausgabe*, begun in 1888 and continuing to this day. It numbers over one hundred volumes. This work is the classic scholarly source for Luther. It typically is abbreviated as "WA" and is quoted in most works on Luther. We can be grateful, however, to Fortress Press for making much of this material available in English. This edition, known as *Luther's Works,* typically abbreviated as "LW," began in 1957 under the initial editorship of Jaroslav Pelikan. It involves numerous translators and editors and includes fifty-five volumes of Luther's writings. Each volume contains helpful introductions.

Purchasing a fifty-five volume set, however, would not be practical for most of us. Other sources fit the bill, including two exceptional compilations. First, Timothy F. Lull's *Martin Luther's Basic Theological Writings* (1989) offers a thorough sampling of Luther's writings. Secondly, not as exhaustive, but quite helpful is John Dillenberger's *Martin Luther: Selections from His Writings* (1962). Each of these two volumes offers an accessible summary of Luther's works. One other book that contains a rewarding sampling of Luther's writings is *By Faith Alone: 365 Devotional Readings Updated in Today's Language* (1998). Four new volumes are a significant addition to English. *The Annotated Luther* presents Luther's key writings alongside of introductions and helpful explanatory notes (Fortress, 2015 and 2016).

Additionally, several separate editions of Luther's writings are available, including *Three Treatises* (Fortress, 1970); *The Large Catechism* (Fortress, 1959); and *The Small Catechism* (Concordia, 1991). Two different volumes of *The Bondage of the Will* are available. *Luther and Erasmus: Free Will and Salvation* (Westminster Press, 1969) makes a worthy edition by including the full text of Erasmus's work that prompted Luther's treatise. *The Bondage of the Will,* translated and introduced by J. I. Packer and O. R. Johnston (Revell, 1957), is also valuable because of the excellent introduction.

If one chapter could be added to this book, it undoubtedly would address Luther's commentaries. These commentaries constitute a majority of his writings and are pivotal to understanding his thought. They are available in a number of volumes in *Luther's Works*. Various commentaries on individual biblical books are also available, including *The Crossway Classic Commentaries: Galatians* (Crossway, 1998); *Luther's Lectures on Romans* (Westminster, 1959); *Romans* (Kregel, 1976); *Peter and Jude* (Kregel, 1990); and *Hebrews* (Kregel, 1980).

Books about Luther

Let's begin by looking at biographies. Roland H. Bainton's *Here I Stand: A Life of Martin Luther* (1977) clearly ranks as one of the most well-known Luther biographies. Bainton's thorough treatment is matched only by his lucid and engaging style. This biography continues to enjoy wide readership decades after its first publication in 1955. Martin Brecht offers the most comprehensive biography of Luther. Originally in German and recently translated into English, his three volumes include *Martin Luther: His Road to Reformation, 1483–1521* (Fortress, 1993); *Shaping and Defining the Reformation, 1521–1532* (1994); and *The Preservation of the Church, 1532–1546* (1999).

Other significant biographies include Peter Manns, *Martin Luther: An Illustrated Biography* (1983); James M. Kittelson, *Luther the Reformer: The Story of the Man and His Career* (1987); Heiko A. Oberman, *Luther: Man Between God and the Devil* (1992). One other book that offers a thorough chronological account, coupled with quotations by Luther and his contemporaries, is Oskar Thulin's *A Life of Luther: Told in Pictures and Narrative by the Reformer and His Contemporaries* (1966). Finally, the magazine *Christian History* has devoted two issues to the life, thought, and times of Luther (Issue 34, 1992, and Issue 39, 1993). One other work that provides helpful portrayals of Luther in his own day and shortly after is Robert Kolb's *Martin Luther as Prophet, Teacher, and Hero: Images of the Reformer, 1520–1620* (1999). Readers of Steven J. Lawson's *Heroic Boldness of Martin Luther* (Reformation Trust, 2013) will be encouraged by the example of Luther's life in this well-told biography.

Other works worth mentioning engage facets of Luther's theology. Alister McGrath offers a helpful discussion of Luther's central ideas in his *Luther's Theology of the Cross* (1985). David C. Steinmetz covers essentially all of the aspects of Luther's thought in *Luther in Context* (1995). Recently translated into English, Bernard Lohse's *Martin Luther's Theology: Its Historical and Systematic Development* (1999) offers a fascinating examination of Luther's work by, as the title indicates, first discussing the historical development, and then secondly arranging his thought in a systematic fashion. Finally, Jaroslav Pelikan offers an enlightening discussion of Luther's translation of the Bible and its impact on the Reformation in *The Reformation of the Bible, The Bible of the Reformation* (1996). This list gives just a sampling of the literature available. All of these works attest to the ongoing relevance of Luther's thought.

Reformation Day, usually observed either on October 31 or the preceding Sunday, offers a fitting time to pay tribute to Martin Luther. This occasion reminds us of his, and the other reformers', role in the history of the Christian tradition. Standing centuries removed from their work, we might do well to make a concerted effort not to forget that role, but rather to turn to these figures and the legacy of their works. Of course, Luther would insist that as we do, we look beyond him and the others to what he and they pointed us to: Christ and the gospel. The prayer given in the Lutheran *Service Book and Hymnal* for Reformation Day may capture this spirit best, as it makes clear why we remember Luther:

> Almighty God, who through the preaching of thy servants, the blessed reformers, hast caused the light of the Gospel to shine forth: Grant, we beseech thee, that knowing its saving power, we may faithfully guard and defend it against all enemies, and joyfully proclaim it, to the salvation of souls and the glory of thy Holy Name; through thy Son, Jesus Christ our Lord, who liveth and reigneth with thee and the Holy Spirit, one God, world without end. Amen.

BIBLIOGRAPHY

Althaus, Paul. *The Theology of Martin Luther.* Philadelphia: Fortress, 1966.

Bainton, Roland H. *Here I Stand: A Life of Martin Luther.* New York: Meridian, 1977.

Brecht, Martin. *Martin Luther: His Road to Reformation, 1483–1521.* Minneapolis: Fortress, 1993.

———. *The Preservation of the Church, 1532–1546.* Minneapolis: Fortress, 1999.

———. *Shaping and Defining the Reformation, 1521–1532.* Minneapolis: Fortress, 1994.

Dillenberger, John. *Martin Luther: Selections from His Writings.* New York: Anchor, 1962.

Dowley, Tim. *Atlas of the European Reformations.* Minneapolis: Fortress, 2015.

Eskew, Harry and Hugh T. McElrath. *Sing with Understanding.* Nashville: Broadman, 1980.

Forde, Gerhard O. *On Being a Theologian of the Cross: Reflections on Luther's Heidelberg Disputation, 1518.* Grand Rapids: Eerdmans, 1997.

Godfrey, W. Robert. *Reformation Sketches: Insights into Luther, Calvin, and the Confessions.* Phillipsburg: P&R, 2003.

Haemig, Mary Jane. *The Annotated Luther: Pastoral Writings, Volume 4.* Minneapolis: Fortress, 2016.

Hustad, Donald. *Jubilate!* Carol Stream, IL: Hope, 1981.

Kerr, Hugh Thomson. *A Compend of Luther's Theology.* Louisville: Westminster, 1943.

Kittelson, James M. *Luther the Reformer: The Story of the Man and His Career.* Minneapolis: Fortress, 1987.

Kolb, Robert. *Martin Luther as Prophet, Teacher, and Hero: Images of the Reformer, 1520–1620.* Grand Rapids: Baker, 1999.

Lawson, Steven J., *The Heroic Boldness of Martin Luther.* Orlando: Reformation Trust, 2013.

Lohse, Bernard. *Martin Luther's Theology: Its Historical and Systematic Development.* Minneapolis: Fortress, 1999.

Lull, Timothy F. *Martin Luther's Basic Theological Writings*. Minneapolis: Fortress, 1989.

Luther, Martin. *Against Hanswurst*. LW 41:179–256.

———. *The Babylonian Captivity of the Church*. LW 36:3–126.

———. *The Bondage of the Will*. Translated by J. I. Packer and O. R. Johnston. Grand Rapids: Revell, 1957.

———. *By Faith Alone: 365 Devotional Readings Updated in Today's Language*. Edited by James C. Galvin. Grand Rapids: World, 1998.

———. *The Complete Sermons of Martin Luther*. 7 volumes. Edited by John Nicholas Lenker (vols. 1–4) and Eugene F. E. Klug (vols. 5–7). Grand Rapids: Baker, 2000.

———. *The Freedom of a Christian*. LW 31:327–77.

———. *Galatians*. Crossway Classic Commentaries. Wheaton: Crossway, 1998.

———. *Hebrews*. Grand Rapids: Kregel, 1980.

———. *The Large Catechism*. Minneapolis: Fortress, 1959.

———. *Luther and Erasmus: Free Will and Salvation*. Edited by Gordon Rupp and Philip S. Watson. Library of Christian Classics. Louisville: Westminster, 1969.

———. *Luther's Lectures on Romans*. Louisville: Westminster, 1959.

———. *Luther's Works*. Edited by Jaroslav Pelikan (vols. 1–30) and Helmut T. Lehmann (vols. 31–55). Minneapolis: Fortress and Concordia.

Vol. 31. *Career of the Reformer*. Edited by Harold J. Grimm. 1957.

Vol. 33. *Career of the Reformer*. Edited by Philip S. Watson. 1955.

Vol. 35. *Word and Sacrament*. Edited by E. Theodore Bachmann. 1960.

Vol. 36. *Word and Sacrament*. Edited by Abdel Ross Wentz. 1959.

Vol. 37. *Word and Sacrament*. Edited by E. Theodore Bachmann. 1960.

Vol. 39. *Church and Ministry*. Edited by Eric W. Gritsch. 1970.

Vol. 40. *Church and Ministry*. Edited by Conrad Bergendoff. 1958.

Vol. 41. *Church and Ministry*. Edited by Eric W. Gritsch. 1966.

Vol. 44. *The Christian in Society*. Edited by James Atkinson. 1966.

Vol. 45. *The Christian in Society*. Edited by Walther I. Brandt. 1962.

Vol. 46. *The Christian in Society*. Edited by Robert C. Schultz. 1967.

Vol. 47. *The Christian in Society*. Edited by Franklin Sherman. 1971.

Vols. 48–50. *Letters*. Edited by Gottfried G. Krodel. 1955.

Vol. 54. *Table Talk*. Edited by Theodore G. Tappert. 1967.

———. *On the Councils and the Church*. LW 41:3–178.

———. *On the Freedom of the Will: A Discourse, in Luther and Erasmus: Free Will and Salvation*. 1969.

————. *On the Papacy in Rome.* LW 39:49–104.

————. *Peter and Jude.* Grand Rapids: Kregel, 1990.

————. *Romans.* Grand Rapids: Kregel, 1976.

————. *The Small Catechism.* St. Louis: Concordia, 1991.

————. *Three Treatises.* Minneapolis: Fortress, 1970.

————. *To the Christian Nobility of the German Nation.* LW 44:115–217.

Manns, Peter. *Martin Luther: An Illustrated Biography.* New York: Crossroad, 1983.

Marius, Richard. *Martin Luther: The Christian Between God and Death.* Cambridge: Harvard University, 1999.

Martin Luther: The Early Years. In *Christian History* 11.2 (1992).

Martin Luther: The Later Years. In *Christian History* 12.3 (1993).

McGrath, Alister E. *Luther's Theology of the Cross: Martin Luther's Theological Breakthrough.* Oxford and Cambridge, MA: Blackwell, 1985.

Nichols, Stephen J. *The Reformation: How a Monk and a Mallet Changed the World.* Wheaton: Crossway, 2007.

Oberman, Heiko A. *Luther: Man Between God and the Devil.* New York: Doubleday, 1992.

Pelikan, Jaroslav. *The Christian Tradition.* Volume 4, *The Reformation of Church and Dogma (1300–1700).* Chicago: University of Chicago, 1984.

————. *The Reformation of the Bible, The Bible of the Reformation.* New Haven: Yale, 1996.

Pettegree, Andrew. *Brand Luther: How an Unheralded Monk Turned His Small Town into a Center of Publishing, Made Himself the Most Famous Man in Europe—and Started the Protestant Reformation.* New York: Penguin, 2015.

Robinson, Paul W. *The Annotated Luther: Church and Sacraments, Volume 3.* Minneapolis: Fortress, 2016.

Sproul, R. C. and Stephen J. Nichols, Editors. *The Legacy of Luther.* Orlando: Reformation Trust, 2016.

Steinmetz, David C. *Luther in Context.* Grand Rapids: Baker, 1995.

Stjerna, Kirsi I. *The Annotated Luther: Word and Faith, Volume 2.* Minneapolis: Fortress, 2015.

Stulken, Marilyn K. *Hymnal Companion to the Lutheran Book of Worship.* Minneapolis: Fortress, 1981.

Thulin, Oskar. *A Life of Luther: Told in Pictures and Narrative by the Reformer and His Contemporaries.* Minneapolis: Fortress, 1966.

Trueman, Carl R. *Luther on the Christian Life: Cross and Freedom.* Wheaton: Crossway, 2015.

Wengert, Timothy W. *The Annotated Luther: The Roots of Reform, Volume 1.* Minneapolis: Fortress, 2015.

INDEX OF PERSONS

Abraham, 50, 96, 218

Adam, 108, 112

Aesop, 55

Agricola, Stephen, 120

Albert of Mainz, 10, 11, 36, 240, 250, 252, 254

Alcibiades, 47

Aleander, 42, 97

Aquinas, Thomas, 72, 246

Aristotle, 31, 34

Atkinson, James, 102

Augustine, 33, 42, 107–9, 112, 134–37, 139, 208

Aurifaber, John, 171–72

Bainton, Roland, 25, 219, 265–66

Bannister, J., 177

Bernard of Clairvaux, 225

Brecht, Martin, 266

Brentius, Joannes, 120

Bruno, Giordano, 59–60

Bucer, Martin, 120, 121

Bugenhagen, Johannes, 60, 87, 98, 141, 216

Bunyan, John, 32, 57

Cajetan, Cardinal, 26, 40, 41, 61, 77, 207

Calvin, John, 56, 70, 125–26, 135, 187, 212

Charlemagne, 89, 134

Charles V, (Emperor), 42–44, 45, 61, 210

Cicero, 63

Cochlaeus, Johannes, 25, 29

Constantine, 133

Cranach, Lucas, 21, 55, 218

de Pres, Josquin, 186–87

Dillenberger, John, 117, 148, 229, 265

Durer, Albrecht, 36, 51

Eck, Johann, 26, 40–41, 56, 61, 77, 206, 207

Edwards, Jonathan, 129–30

Elijah, 64

Elisha, 64

Elizabeth, 50

Emerson, Ralph Waldo, 25

Erasmus, Desiderius, 17, 55, 97, 104–117, 169, 265

Erikson, Erik, 172

Esau, 52

Eskew, Harry, 196, 197

Fischer, Robert H., 132

Forde, Gerhard O., 85

Frederick, John, 54, 140, 210

Frederick the Wise, (Elector of Saxony), 31, 40, 42, 44, 45, 52, 54, 60, 120, 141, 169, 185, 210, 216

Gaffin Jr., Richard, 160
Grimm, Harold J., 102
Gritsch, Eric W., 212

Henry of Braunschweig/
    Wolfenbuttel, (Duke),
    210–11
Henry VIII, 98
Holbein, Hans, 19, 49
Holland, William, 58
Horace, 123
Hus, John, 17, 30, 40, 202
Hustad, Donald, 197

Joachim of Brandenburg,
    (Margrave), 173
John, 110
John the Baptist, 64
Johnston, O. R., 117, 265
Jonas, Justas, 60, 120
Jorg, Junker, 44, 45, 66

Karlstadt, Andreas, 40, 47, 60, 90,
    125
Kerr, Hugh Thomson, 85
Knox, John, 212
Kolb, Robert, 266
Koppe, Leonard, 50, 199
Krodel, Gottfried G., 66

Lang, Johann, 107
Laurence, (Saint), 252–53
Lauterbach, Anthony, 169
Leo III, (Pope), 89, 134
Leo X, (Pope), 10, 26, 35–37, 41,
    44, 88, 98, 100, 102, 250,
    258
Leupold, Ulrich S., 197
Lohse, Bernard, 84, 266
Lombard, Peter, 33
Luder, Hans, (Luther's father),
    27, 30

Luder, Margaret, (Luther's
    mother), 27
Luder, Martin, 26
Lull, Timothy F., 85, 117, 132,
    147, 167, 212, 229
Luther, Elizabeth, (Luther's
    daughter), 53, 175
Luther, Hans, (Luther's son), 140,
    151, 166, 189
Luther, Katie, (Luther's wife). See
    von Bora, Katherina
Luther, Magdalena, (Luther's
    daughter), 21, 53, 151, 166
Luther, Martin
    birth, 26
    childhood and early education,
        26–28
    decision to become a monk,
        20, 23, 26, 30
    monastery life, 20, 30–31, 62
    education at University of
        Wittenberg, 26, 31–32
    teaching at Wittenberg, 17–18,
        31–33, 59–61
    posting of Ninety-Five Theses,
        9–11, 15, 17, 23, 33,
        35–36, 42, 49, 88, 152,
        179, 189, 232
    conversion, 37–39
    debates, Cardinal Cajetan, 26,
        40, 61, 77, 207
        Johann Eck, 26, 40–41, 56,
        61, 77, 206–7
    Diet of Worms, 20, 23, 26, 42–44,
        49, 179, 185, 187, 188, 206
    exile at Wartburg Castle, 20,
        23, 26, 44–45, 48, 55,
        65–66, 64, 188–89
    return to Wittenberg, 45, 47,
        48, 55, 152

marriage, 49–52

family life, 52–54, 140, 151, 169–77

plague of 1527, 140–43, 189

theological views, of the cross, 72–76

   solas, 76–82

   laity, 82–84

   sacraments, 95–98, Lord's Supper, 119–31

debates with Erasmus, 105–17

death, 16, 63–64

Luther, Martin, (Luther's son), 175

Manns, Peter, 266

Martha, 205

Mary, 205

Mary, (Jesus' mother), 252, 257

McElrath, Hugh, 196, 197

McGrath, Alister E., 85, 266

Melanchthon, Philip, 47, 60–61, 64, 120, 152, 169, 174, 177

Michelangelo, 36

Moses, 73, 81, 159, 216

Muenzer, Thomas, 144–45

Nietzsche, Friedrich, 19

Noll, Mark, 75

Oberman, Heiko A., 266

Oecolampadius, John, 120, 123

Osiander, Andreas, 120

Packer, J. I., 104, 117, 265

Paschal I, (Pope), 244–45

Paul, 33, 34, 39, 75, 76, 90, 99, 101, 108, 110, 112, 113, 128, 129, 153, 212, 227

Pelagius, 108, 109, 114

Pelikan, Jaroslav, 264, 267

Peter, 90, 224

Phillip of Hesse, 57, 119, 120, 122

Raphael, 36

Rhau, Georg, 186

Rupp, E. Gordon, 117

Samson, 51

Schwerdgeburth, 177

Severinus, (Pope), 244–45

Socrates, 47

Spalatin, George, 60

Steinmetz, David C., 85, 266

Stulken, Marilyn K., 197

Tappert, Theodore G., 66

Tetzel, 36, 37, 231, 238–56

Thomas á Kempis, 27

Thulin, Oskar, 66, 266

Timothy, 153, 212

Virgil, 63

von Bora, Katherina, 21, 48, 52–54, 57, 63, 140, 169, 170, 175, 180

von Staupitz, Johann, 31–32, 38

Walther, Johann, 186, 188, 196

Watson, Philip S., 117

Watts, Isaac, 192, 196

Weller, Jerome, 169

Wentz, Abdel Ross, 102

Wesley, Charles, 58–59

Wesley, John, 59

Wycliffe, John, 17, 40

Zechariah, 50

Zwingli, Ulrich, 23, 57, 67, 96, 106, 120–27, 130, 135, 140, 187

INDEX OF LUTHER'S WORKS

ABC Book for Children, 157

Address to the Christian Nobility of the German Nation (1520), 87–93, 98, 134, 135

Admonition to Peace Based on the Twelve Articles of the Peasants of Swabia (1525), 135, 145

"The Adoration of the Sacrament" (1523), 123

Aesop's Fables (German translation), 55–56, 154

Against Hanswurst (1541), 204, 210–12

Against the Detestable Bull of the Antichrist (1520), 41, 98

Against the Robbing and Murdering Bands of Peasants (1525), 135, 146

Augsburg Confession (1530), 48, 61

The Babylonian Captivity of the Church (1520), 60, 83, 87, 88, 93–95, 98, 102, 122, 124, 141

The Blessed Sacrament of the Holy and True Body and Blood of Christ (1519), 124

The Bondage of the Will (1525), 20, 48, 54–55, 67, 103–17, 153, 265

By Faith Alone: 365 Devotional Readings Updated in Today's Language (1998), 265

"Christ Jesus Lay in Death's Strong Bands" (1524), 194

A Compend of Luther's Theology (1943), 85

The Complete Sermons of Martin Luther (2000), 228–29

Concerning Music, 184

"Concerning the Order of Public Worship" (1523), 166, 201–5, 217

Confession Concerning Christ's Supper (1528), 119–32, 137

"Dear Christians, One and All, Rejoice" (1523), 190–92

Dr. Martin Luther's Warning to His Dear German People (1531), 135

The Estate of Marriage (1522), 135

Explanations of the Ninety-Five Theses (1518), 94, 236, 238

The Freedom of the Christian (1520), 88, 98–102, 144

"From Trouble Deep, I Cry to Thee" (1523), 192–93

Galatians, 57–59, 78–79, 265

German Bible (1534), 48, 54–55, 77, 218

German Catechism. See The Large Catechism

The German Mass (1526), 48, 188, 197
German New Testament (1522), 45, 55, 152

Hebrews, 265
Heidelberg Disputation (1518), 72, 80, 81, 260

"In the Midst of Life" (1524), 193

Judgment of Martin Luther on Monastic Vows (1521), 30, 50

The Large Catechism (1529), 56, 61–62, 129, 130, 153, 160, 167, 265
Luther and Erasmus: Free Will and Salvation (1969), 117, 265
Luther's Lectures on Romans (1959), 265
Luther's Works, 65, 66, 102, 117, 131, 147, 181, 197, 212, 228, 264, 265

Martin Luther: Selections from His Writings (1962), 117, 148, 229, 265
Martin Luther's Basic Theological Writings (1989), 85, 117, 132, 148, 167, 213, 229, 264
"A Mighty Fortress Is Our God" (1527), 15, 21, 48, 139, 183, 184, 188–91

"A New Song Shall Here Be Begun" (1523), 48, 185–86, 195
Ninety-Five Theses (1517), 11, 17, 23, 26, 33, 35–37, 38, 40, 42, 49, 67, 72, 88, 93, 94, 122, 143–44, 152, 179, 189, 232–61

On Temporal Authority: To What Extent Should It Be Obeyed (1523), 48, 135, 137–40, 148

On the Councils and the Church (1539), 21, 149, 162–63, 199–213
On the Jews and Their Lies (1543), 62
On the Papacy in Rome (1520), 204, 212
An Open Letter on the Harsh Book Against the Peasants (1525), 135, 146
"An Order of Mass and Communion for the Church at Wittenberg" (1523), 187–88

Peter and Jude, 265

Receiving Both Kinds in the Sacrament (1522), 124
Romans, 57, 59, 82, 265

The Sacrament of the Body and Blood of Christ—Against the Fanatics (1526), 124
"A Sermon on How to Contemplate Christ's Holy Sufferings" (1519), 21, 221–29
"Sermon on Indulgences and Grace" (1518), 260
"A Sermon on the Estate of Marriage" (1519), 135
Smalcald Articles (1529), 48, 61–62, 80
The Small Catechism (1529), 20, 48, 56, 61–62, 94–95, 103–4, 128–29, 147, 149, 151–67, 201, 265
Spiritual Hymn Booklet (1524), 196

"Table Talk," 18, 20, 52, 53–54, 66, 75–76, 113, 116–17, 164–66, 169–181, 186–87, 203, 215, 217, 263
"This Is My Body" (1527), 124
"Thou Art Three in Unity" (1543), 195

Three Treatises (1520), 20, 26, 41,
   67, 87–102, 135, 265
Tischreden. See "Table Talk"
"Two Kinds of Righteousness"
   (1519), 78

Weimar Ausgabe, 65, 264
Whether One May Flee from a
   Deadly Plague (1527), 135, 138,
   141, 147–48
Wittenberg Edition (Latin), 48, 63

INDEX OF SCRIPTURE

Genesis
12–15—96
17—96
22—218, 219

Exodus—73–74
20—159–60
25:22—73
33—73

Psalms—17, 26, 33,
    34, 38, 77, 187,
    190, 192, 203, 209
14—113
68:20—64
130—192

Jeremiah
6:14—260

Matthew
1:1—106
4:17—236
10:39—75
16:16–19—244
18—209
20:16—252
26:26–28—128

Mark
14:22–24—128

Luke
10—205
10:25–37—248
10:27—136
22:19–20—128

John
3:16—64
6:44—108
15:1—124
15:16—108
16:8—113

Acts—130
2:36–37—224
15—206

Romans—17, 26, 33,
    34, 37–38, 57,
    58, 77
1—99, 112
1:17—39
3:10–11—113
3:25—73–74
5:12–21—108
6–7—238
8—75
10:4—82

1 Corinthians
1—74
2:2—193
9:19—99

11:23–25—128
11:27–29—129
12—257
12:28—256

Galatians—17, 26,
    33, 34, 38, 57, 77

Philippians
2—101

Colossians
2:14—227

1 Timothy
2:5—76, 81

2 Timothy
2:2—153
4:2—212

Hebrews—17, 26, 33,
    34, 38, 77

James
3:1—256
5:16—163

1 Peter
2:5—82
2:9—90
5:10—99

Revelation
17—211

TAKE A GUIDED TOUR
THROUGH CHURCH HISTORY

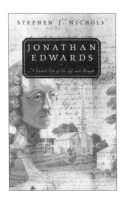  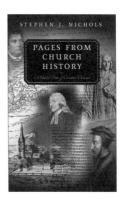

THE GUIDED TOUR series offers basic introductions to the life and writings of significant figures of church history. Learn about these godly men and women as you hear them speak for themselves.

Anne Bradstreet, Heidi L. Nichols

George Whitefield, James L. Schwenk

J. Gresham Machen, Stephen J. Nichols

Jonathan Edwards, Stephen J. Nichols

Katherine Parr, Brandon G. Withrow

Pages from Church History, Stephen J. Nichols

Princeton Seminary (1812–1929), Gary Steward

Thomas Manton, Derek Cooper

Stephen J. Nichols (PhD, Westminster Theological Seminary) is President of Reformation Bible College and Chief Academic Officer of Ligonier Ministries. He hosts the weekly podcast *5 Minutes in Church History*.